تَسْهِيْلُ النَّحْوِ

TASHEEL AL-NAHW

Version 2.2

تَسْهِيْلُ النَّحْوِ

TASHEEL AL-NAHW
Version 2.2

based on

'Ilm al-Nahw of Mawlana Mushtaq Ahmad Charthawali

Prepared by
Aamir Bashir

TABLE OF CONTENTS

CHAPTER 4   109

الْعَوَامِلُ – Governing Words

LIST OF TABLES

ACKNOWLEDGMENTS

The people who have helped to make this project a success cannot all be mentioned by name. However, I must single out Sr. A. Naviwala who typed up the old *Tasheel al-Nahw*, and thus helped to kick-start the project; the students and instructors at Darul Uloom al-Madania's eAlim program; First year students at Darul Uloom al-Madania (academic years 2010–2011 and 2011–2012); and Mawlana Omar Salejee of Madrasa In'amiyya South Africa. I have greatly benefitted from their valuable feedback and suggesstions and help with proof-reading. May Allah reward them, and all others for their contributions and help.

بسم الله الرحمن الرحيم

نحمده و نصلي على رسوله الكريم

FOREWORD

This is version 2.2 of the revised *Tasheel al-Nahw*, which in turn is an expanded translation of the Urdu language primer of Arabic grammar, *'Ilm al-Nahw* by Mawlana Mushtaq Ahmad Charthawali. Mawlana Charthawali's primers for *Nahw* (Arabic grammar) and *Sarf* (Arabic Morphology) are standard textbooks in Western *madrasahs*. The original English translation of *'Ilm al-Nahw* titled *Tasheel al-Nahw* was prepared by scholars from Madrasah Islamiyyah, Benoni, South Africa. As great as that effort was, it suffered from several issues especially with regards to language and clarity of the English and Arabic texts. In 2010, I decided to bring out a revised edition of this translation to address these issues. During the course of this revision, I consulted various grammar works including *al-Nahw al-Wadih*, *Sharh ibn 'Aqil*, *Mu'jam al-Qawa'id al-'Arabiyyah*, and *A Simplified Arabic Grammar*. I completely revised some sections, as well as a number of definitions. I also changed the organization in a way that I felt would make it easier for students to understand how each section fits in the overall picture.

Since then, I have had a chance to teach this book many times and every such occasion has led to further revisions and improvements. This latest version is vastly different from the original edition that I published online in 2011. Many sections have been modified, some have been completely revised, confusing sentences have been elaborated, more examples and exercises have been added, including many from *al-Nahw al-Wadih* and *Mu'allim al-Insha'*, and where needed, the relevant *al-Nahw al-Wadih* section has been pointed out in the footnotes. These footnotes are for the benefit of the teachers. The students can choose to ignore them. Lastly, an appendix has been attached at the end, identifying *Tasheel al-Nahw*'s place in *Nahw* texts, as well as suggesting a possible curriculum of classical Arabic studies.

This is a beginner-to-intermediate level text; therefore, I have not transliterated Arabic words exactly, keeping in mind that most people at this stage will not be comfortable with Arabic transliteration schemes. Rather, I have used approximate equivalents that are easier to read for the untrained. Nevertheless, non-English words have been italicized to reflect their non-English origin. The documentation in the foot-notes does not follow any particular academic standard; rather, it has been kept simple for ease of students. It should also be noted that the English equivalents of Arabic grammar terms are mere approximations. In some cases, they convey the exact meaning. In many cases, they do not. The student is, therefore, urged to focus on the original term in Arabic.

I would also like to point out that this is not a do-it-yourself text. First of all, it assumes some prior knowledge of Arabic such as that acquired through studying *Ten Lessons of Arabic* and/or *Durus al-Lughah al-'Arabiyyah* vol. 1. Moreover, it needs to be studied with a teacher.

However, it can be used as a revision text by those who have already studied *Nahw* using other texts. It is respectfully suggested to the teachers of this text to also use *al-Nahw al-Wadih* (all six volumes) as reference and for additional examples and exercises, as and when needed. Moreover, it should also be pointed out that this is not an exhaustive text. It does not cover every issue of *Nahw*, in brief or in detail. It is assumed that the student will be studying relatively advanced *Nahw* texts (such as *Hidayat al-Nahw* or *al-Nahw al-Wadih*) after this to round off his/her training of *Nahw*. The sample curriculum given in the appendix can be used for that purpose.

To the best of my ability, I have tried to remove all errors. However, as is the case with all human endeavors, there are bound to be some mistakes in it, and definitely, room for improvement. Your comments, constructive criticism, and suggestions are all welcome. You can contact me with your feedback at the email address given at the end.

I hope and pray that this latest version will be of benefit to the students. I also pray that Allah Most High accepts this humble effort from all those who have contributed to it in any way, and gives us the power to continue with more. I also request the readers and all those who benefit from it in any way to remember me in their prayers.

And He alone gives success.

وَصَلَّى اللهُ تَعَالَى عَلَى خَيْرِ خَلْقِهِ سَيِّدِنَا وَمَوْلَانَا مُحَمَّدٍ وَّعَلَى أَلِهِ وَأَصْحَابِهِ أَجْمَعِيْنَ

Aamir Bashir
Chicago, IL
26th Safar, 1438 (26th November, 2016)
E-mail: ainbay97@gmail.com

الْاِصْطِلَاحَاتُ الْعَرَبِيَّة

ARABIC TERMS

Arabic Term	Approximate Transliteration	Equivalent English Term / Description of the meaning
اِسْمٌ	ism	Noun
فِعْلٌ	fi'l	Verb
حَرْفٌ	harf	Particle
مُذَكَّرٌ	mudhakkar	Masculine
مُؤَنَّثٌ	mu'annath	Feminine
وَاحِدٌ	waahid	Singular
تَثْنِيَةٌ	tathniyah	Dual
جَمْعٌ	jam'	Plural
ضَمَّةٌ	dammah	ـُ
فَتْحَةٌ	fathah	ـَ
كَسْرَةٌ	kasrah	ـِ
حَرَكَةٌ جَمْعٌ: حَرَكَاتٌ	harakah plural: harakaat	Short vowels, i.e., *dammah* ـُ, *fathah* ـَ, *kasrah* ـِ
حُرُوفُ الْعِلَّةِ	huroof al-'illah	Long vowels i.e., و ـ ا ـ ي
إِعْرَابٌ	i'raab	These are the variations at the end of the word which take place in accordance with the governing word.
تَنْوِيْنٌ	tanween	two *fathahs* (ـً), two *dammahs* (ـٌ), two *kasrahs* (ـٍ)
سُكُوْنٌ	sukoon	ـْ
سَاكِنٌ	saakin	A letter with *sukoon*
تَشْدِيْدٌ	tashdeed	ـّ
مُشَدَّدٌ	mushaddad	A letter with *tashdeed*
فَاعِلٌ	faa'il	Subject i.e. the doer
مَفْعُوْلٌ	maf'ool	Object i.e. the person or thing upon whom or which the work is done.
عَامِلٌ	'aamil	Governing word i.e. a word which causes *i'raab* change in the word(s) following it.

xiii

Arabic Term	Approximate Transliteration	Equivalent English Term / Description of the meaning
مَعْمُوْلٌ	*ma'mool*	The governed word i.e. a word in which the *i'raab* change occurred.
فِعْلٌ مَعْرُوْفٌ	*fi'l ma'roof*	The active verb i.e. a verb whose doer is known/mentioned.
فِعْلٌ مَجْهُوْلٌ	*fi'l majhool*	The passive verb i.e. a verb whose doer is not known/mentioned.
فِعْلٌ لَازِمٌ	*fi'l laazim*	The intransitive verb i.e. a verb which can be understood without a مَفْعُوْلٌ.
اَلْفِعْلُ الْمُتَعَدِّيْ	*fi'l muta'addi*	The transitive verb i.e. a verb which cannot be fully understood without a مَفْعُوْلٌ.
مَعْرِفَةٌ	*ma'rifah*	Definite noun. It is generally indicated by an ال. For example, اَلْبَيْتُ <u>the</u> house (a particular/specific house).
نَكِرَةٌ	*nakirah*	Indefinite noun. It is generally indicated by a *tanween*. e.g. بَيْتٌ <u>a</u> house (any house).
مَرْفُوْعٌ	*marfoo'*	It is a word which is in the state of رَفْعٌ. It is generally represented by a *dammah* on the last letter.
مَنْصُوْبٌ	*mansoob*	It is a word which is in the state of نَصْبٌ. It is generally represented by a *fathah* on the last letter.
مَجْرُوْرٌ	*majroor*	It is a word which is in the state of جَرٌّ. It is generally represented by a *kasrah* on the last letter.

CHAPTER 1

Section 1.1

اَلنَّحْوُ – Arabic Grammar

Definition:

Nahw is a science, which teaches us how to join a noun, verb or particle to form a correct sentence, as well as what the إِعْرَابٌ (condition) of the last letter of a word should be.

Subject Matter:

Its subject matter is كَلِمَةٌ (word) and كَلَامٌ (sentence).

Objective:

- The immediate objective is to learn how to read, write and speak Arabic correctly, and to avoid making mistakes in this. For example, زَيْد, دَار, دَخَلَ, and فِي are four words. The science of *Nahw* teaches us how to put them together to form a correct sentence.

- The mid-term objective is to use our Arabic skills to understand the *Qur'an*, *Hadeeth*, *Fiqh* and other Islamic sciences, so that we can act upon them.

- The ultimate objective through the above is to gain the pleasure of Allah Most High.

Section 1.2
اَلْكَلِمَةُ – The word

Any word uttered by humans is called a لَفْظٌ. If it has a meaning, it is called مَوْضُوعٌ (meaningful); and if it does not have any meaning, it is called مُهْمَلٌ (meaningless).

In Arabic, لَفْظٌ مَوْضُوعٌ (meaningful word) is of two types: مُفْرَدٌ and مُرَكَّبٌ.

1. مُفْرَدٌ – Single: It is a single word such as كِتَابٌ (book). Such a word is also called كَلِمَةٌ.

2. مُرَكَّبٌ – Compound: It is a group of two or more words, which may form a complete or an incomplete sentence such as طَالِبٌ ذَكِيٌّ (intelligent student) or اَلطَّالِبُ ذَكِيٌّ (The student is intelligent.).

Types of كَلِمَةٌ

There are three types of كَلِمَةٌ:

1. اِسْمٌ (noun)

2. فِعْلٌ (verb)

3. حَرْفٌ (particle)

اِسْمٌ – Noun:

- Classical definition: It is a كَلِمَةٌ whose meaning can be understood without the need to combine it with another word, and it does not have a tense.[1]

- Modern definition: It is the name of a person, place or thing.[2]

  Examples: رَجُلٌ a man

  اَلْبَيْتُ the house

Notes:

- Since this textbook is designed for classical Arabic; therefore, throughout the rest of the book, اِسْمٌ will be used in the sense of its classical definition.

- An اِسْمٌ can never have a تَنْوِيْنٌ (tanween) and an ال at the same time.

---

[1] Ibn 'Aqil expresses this is as follows: اَلْكَلِمَةُ إِنْ دَلَّتْ عَلَى مَعْنًى فِي نَفْسِهَا غَيْرَ مُقْتَرِنٍ بِزَمَانٍ فَهِيَ اسْمٌ. See 'Abdullah ibn 'Aqil, *Sharh ibn 'Aqil 'ala Alfiyyat ibn Malik* (Cairo: Dar al-Turath, 1980), vol. 1, 15.

[2] This is the definition given in *al-Nahw al-Wadih*. The Arabic reads: اَلِاسْمُ: كُلُّ لَفْظٍ يُسَمَّى بِهِ إِنْسَانٌ أَوْ حَيَوَانٌ أَوْ نَبَاتٌ أَوْ جَمَادٌ أَوْ أَيُّ شَيْءٍ آخَرَ. See 'Ali al-Jaarim & Mustafa Ameen, *al-Nahw al-Wadih li al-Madaris al-Ibtida'iyyah* (Cairo: Dar al-Ma'arif, n.d.), vol. 1, 16.

فِعْلٌ – Verb:

- Classical definition: It is a كَلِمَةٌ whose meaning can be understood without the need to combine it with another word, and it has one of the three tenses: past, present, or future.[3]

- Modern definition: It denotes an action.[4]

    Examples: ضَرَبَ   He hit.   نَصَرَ   He helped.

Notes:

- Since this textbook is designed for classical Arabic; therefore, throughout the rest of the book, فِعْلٌ will be used in the sense of its classical definition.

- A فِعْلٌ can never have a تَنْوِيْنٌ (*tanween*) or an ال.

حَرْفٌ – Particle:

It is a كَلِمَةٌ whose meaning cannot be understood without joining an اِسْمٌ or a فِعْلٌ or both to it.

    e.g.   مِنْ   (from)

            عَلٰى   (on top)

EXERCISES

1. State with reason whether the following words are حَرْفٌ ، فِعْلٌ or اِسْمٌ.

    i.   جَلَسَ   (He sat.)   iii.   بِنْتٌ   (girl)

    ii.   وَ   (and)   iv.   كَسَرَ   (He broke.)

2. Find the meaning and the plural of the following أَسْمَاء using a dictionary.

    i.   قَلَمٌ   iii.   كِتَابٌ

    ii.   فَصْلٌ   iv.   سَبُّوْرَةٌ

---

[3] See *Sharh ibn 'Aqil*, vol. 1, 15.

[4] See *al-Nahw al-Wadih, Ibtida'iyyah*, vol. 1, 16.

Section 1.3

أَقْسَامُ الاِسْمِ – Types of *ism*

اِسْمٌ is of three types:

1. جَامِدٌ – Primary *ism*: It is an اِسْمٌ which is neither derived from another word nor is any word derived from it.

   e.g.   فَرَسٌ   horse   بِنْتٌ   girl

2. مَصْدَرٌ – Root *ism*: It is an اِسْمٌ from which many words are derived.

   e.g.   ضَرْبٌ   to hit   نَصْرٌ   to help

3. مُشْتَقٌّ – Derived *ism*: It is an اِسْمٌ which is derived from a مَصْدَرٌ.

   e.g.   ضَارِبٌ   hitter   مَنْصُوْرٌ   one who is helped

أَقْسَامُ الْفِعْلِ – Types of *fiʿl*

فِعْلٌ is of four types:

1.	الْمَاضِيْ	Past tense	e.g.	ضَرَبَ	He hit.
2.	الْمُضَارِعُ	Present and Future tense	e.g.	يَضْرِبُ	He is hitting or will hit.
3.	الْأَمْرُ	Positive Command/ Imperative	e.g.	اِضْرِبْ	Hit!
4.	النَّهْيُ	Negative Command/ Prohibitive	e.g.	لَا تَضْرِبْ	Don't hit!

أَقْسَامُ الْحَرْفِ – Types of particle

حَرْفٌ is of two types:

1. عَامِلٌ – Causative Particle: It is a حَرْفٌ which causes إِعْرَابٌ change in the word after it.

   e.g.   زَيْدٌ فِي الْمَسْجِدِ   Zayd is in the mosque.

2. غَيْرُ الْعَامِلِ – Non-Causative: It is a حَرْفٌ which does not cause إِعْرَابٌ change in the word after it.

   e.g.   ثُمَّ   then   وَ   and

EXERCISES

1. Correct the following words (stating a reason) and give their meanings.

   i.   اَلْبَيْتٌ   iii.   اَلْوَرَقٌ

   ii.   اَلْفَتَحَ   iv.   سَمِعٌ

2. Find the meanings and the plurals of the following *isms* using a dictionary.

   i.   بُسْتَانٌ   iii.   بَابٌ

   ii.   قَمَرٌ   iv.   كَلْبٌ

3. Translate the following sentences, and identify the different types of *fi'ls* in them.

   i.   فَتَحَ خَالِدُنِ الشُّبَّاكَ   iii.   اُكْتُبْ رِسَالَةً

   ii.   يَدْرُسُ أَحْمَدُ فِي الْمَدْرَسَةِ   iv.   لَا تَقْرَأْ ذٰلِكَ الْكِتَابَ

Section 1.4

اَلْجُمَلُ وَ الْمُرَكَّبَاتُ – Sentences and phrases

مُرَكَّبٌ is of two types: مُرَكَّبٌ مُفِيدٌ and مُرَكَّبٌ غَيْرُ مُفِيدٍ.

- مُرَكَّبٌ مُفِيدٌ is also called جُمْلَةٌ مُفِيدَةٌ and مُرَكَّبٌ تَامٌّ, كَلَامٌ تَامٌّ. It is a complete sentence. Often, it is just called كَلَامٌ.

- مُرَكَّبٌ غَيْرُ مُفِيدٍ is also called جُمْلَةٌ غَيْرُ مُفِيدَةٍ, مُرَكَّبٌ نَاقِصٌ and كَلَامٌ نَاقِصٌ. It is an incomplete sentence.

From now on, when I use "sentence," I will be referring to a complete sentence; and when I use "phrase," I will be referring to an incomplete sentence.

Types of sentences

There are two types of sentences:

A. جُمْلَةٌ خَبَرِيَّةٌ: It is a sentence which has the possibility of being true or false.

B. جُمْلَةٌ إِنْشَائِيَّةٌ: It is a sentence which does not have the possibility of being true or false.

Section 1.4.1

أَقْسَامُ الجُمْلَةِ الخَبَرِيَّةِ

جُمْلَةٌ خَبَرِيَّةٌ is of two types:

1. جُمْلَةٌ اسْمِيَّةٌ خَبَرِيَّةٌ – Nominal sentence:

   <u>Definition:</u> It is a sentence which begins with an اِسْمٌ.

   - The second part of the sentence can be an اِسْمٌ or a فِعْلٌ.
   - The first part of the sentence is called مُبْتَدَأٌ (subject) or مُسْنَدٌ إِلَيْهِ (the word about which information is being given).
   - The second part of the sentence is called خَبَرٌ (predicate) or مُسْنَدٌ (the word giving the information).
   - The مُبْتَدَأٌ is generally مَعْرِفَةٌ and the خَبَرٌ generally نَكِرَةٌ.
   - Both parts (خَبَرٌ and مُبْتَدَأٌ) are مَرْفُوعٌ.

Sentence Analysis

| اَلْبَيْتُ | نَظِيفٌ | The house is clean. |
| مُبْتَدَأٌ | خَبَرٌ | + | = | جُمْلَةٌ اسْمِيَّةٌ خَبَرِيَّةٌ |

6

Note: A sentence may have more than one خَبَر.

Sentence Analysis

قَوِيٌّ   طَوِيلٌ   اَلرَّجُلُ   The man is tall and strong.

جُمْلَةٌ اِسْمِيَّةٌ خَبَرِيَّةٌ = + خَبَرٌ 1 + خَبَرٌ 2 + مُبْتَدَأٌ

2. جُمْلَةٌ فِعْلِيَّةٌ خَبَرِيَّةٌ – Verbal sentence:

<u>Definition:</u> It is a sentence which begins with a فِعْلٌ.

- The first part of the sentence is called فِعْلٌ or مُسْنَدٌ.
- The second part of the sentence is called فَاعِلٌ or مُسْنَدٌ إِلَيْهِ and is always مَرْفُوعٌ.

Sentence Analysis

زَيْدٌ   جَلَسَ   Zayd sat.

جُمْلَةٌ فِعْلِيَّةٌ خَبَرِيَّةٌ = فَاعِلٌ + فِعْلٌ

Note: In the above example, the فِعْلٌ is اَلْفِعْلُ اللَّازِمُ i.e. it is a فِعْلٌ whose meaning can be understood without a مَفْعُولٌ.

Note: If the فِعْلٌ is اَلْفِعْلُ الْمُتَعَدِّي i.e. a فِعْلٌ whose meaning cannot be fully understood without a مَفْعُولٌ, then a مَفْعُولٌ will be added and it will be مَنْصُوبٌ.

Sentence Analysis

السَّمَاءَ   اللهُ   خَلَقَ   Allah created the sky.

جُمْلَةٌ فِعْلِيَّةٌ خَبَرِيَّةٌ = مَفْعُولٌ + فَاعِلٌ + فِعْلٌ

EXERCISES[5]

1. Translate, fill in the *i'raab*, and analyze the following sentences.

iii. فتح محمد الباب   ii. البستان جميل   i. المعلم حاضر

vi. الرجل وقف   v. وقف الرجل   iv. المدرسة كبيرة نظيفة

2. What is the difference between (v) and (vi) above?

---

[5] For more examples and exercises, please refer to *al-Nahw al-Wadih, Ibtida'iyyah*, vol. 1, 11-19 & 36-46.

Section 1.4.2

جُمْلَةٌ إِنْشَائِيَّةٌ is of ten types:

1.	اَلْأَمْرُ	Positive Command	e.g.	اِضْرِبْ	Hit!
2.	اَلنَّهْيُ	Negative Command	e.g.	لَا تَضْرِبْ	Don't Hit!
3.	اَلْاِسْتِفْهَامُ	Interrogative	e.g.	هَلْ ضَرَبَ زَيْدٌ؟	Did Zayd hit?
4.	اَلتَّمَنِّي	Desire	e.g.	لَيْتَ الشَّبَابَ عَائِدٌ!	I wish youth would return.

Note: لَيْتَ is generally used for something unattainable.

5.	اَلتَّرَجِّي	Hope	e.g.	لَعَلَّ الْاِمْتِحَانَ سَهْلٌ	Hopefully, the examination will be easy.

Note: لَعَلَّ is generally used for something attainable.

6.	اَلنِّدَاءُ	Exclamation	e.g.	يَا اَللهُ!	O Allah!
7.	اَلْعَرْضُ	Request/Offer	e.g.	أَلَا تَأْتِينِي فَأُعْطِيَكَ دِينَارًا؟	Will you not come to me so that I may give you a *dinar*?

Note: اَلْعَرْضُ is a mere request; no answer is anticipated.

8.	اَلْقَسَمُ	Oath	e.g.	وَاللهِ!	By Allah!
9.	اَلتَّعَجُّبُ	Amazement	e.g.	مَا أَحْسَنَ زَيْدًا!	How good Zayd is!
10.	اَلْعُقُودُ	Transaction	e.g.	The seller says بِعْتُ هٰذَا الْكِتَابَ – I sold this book. and the buyer says اِشْتَرَيْتُهُ – I bought it.	

Note: The sentences for اَلْعُقُودُ are in reality خَبَرِيَّةٌ. However, Islamic law recognizes them as إِنْشَائِيَّةٌ with respect to all contracts, and requires that they (past tense verbal sentences) be used to convey definiteness.

Sentence Analysis:

زَيْدٌ؟   ضَرَبَ   هَلْ   Did Zayd hit?

حَرْفُ الْاِسْتِفْهَامِ + فِعْلٌ + فَاعِلٌ = جُمْلَةٌ إِنْشَائِيَّةٌ

EXERCISE

1. State what type of جُمْلَةٌ إِنْشَائِيَّةٌ are the following sentences.

    i. يَا إِبْرَاهِيمُ!   iii. كَيْفَ حَالُكَ؟

    ii. اِسْمَعْ   iv. لَا تَدْخُلْ

أَقْسَامُ الْمُرَكَّبِ النَّاقِصِ – Types of phrases

Phrases are of five types:

1. اَلْمُرَكَّبُ التَّوْصِيفِيُّ – Descriptive phrase:[6] It is a phrase in which one word describes the other.

   - The describing word is called صِفَةٌ.
   - The object being described is called مَوْصُوْفٌ.
   - The مَوْصُوْفٌ and صِفَةٌ must correspond in four things:
     1. إِعْرَابٌ.
     2. Gender i.e. being masculine or feminine.
     3. Number i.e. being singular, dual or plural.
     4. Being مَعْرِفَةٌ or نَكِرَةٌ.

   For example,

صَالِحٌ	رَجُلٌ	a righteous man
صِفَةٌ	مَوْصُوْفٌ	

الْعَاقِلَةُ	اَلْبِنْتُ	the intelligent/wise girl
صِفَةٌ	مَوْصُوْفٌ	

2. اَلْمُرَكَّبُ الْإِضَافِيُّ – Possessive phrase: It is a phrase in which the first word (مُضَافٌ) is attributed to the second one (مُضَافٌ إِلَيْهِ). In some cases, this means that the second word owns or possesses the first.

   - The مُضَافٌ never gets an ال or a تَنْوِيْنٌ.
   - The مُضَافٌ إِلَيْهِ is always مَجْرُوْرٌ. The
     e.g.

زَيْدٍ	كِتَابُ	Zayd's book
مُضَافٌ إِلَيْهِ	مُضَافٌ	

   - The إِعْرَابٌ of the مُضَافٌ will be according to the عَامِلٌ governing it. For example,

زَيْدٍ	كِتَابَ	وَجَدْتُ	I found Zayd's book.
مُضَافٌ إِلَيْهِ	مُضَافٌ		
مَفْعُوْلٌ بِهِ		فِعْلٌ مَعَ فَاعِلِهِ	

---

[6] For more examples and exercises, please refer to *al-Nahw al-Wadih*, *Ibtida'iyyah*, vol. 1, 82-86.

Notes:

1. Sometimes many مُضَافٌ and مُضَافٌ إِلَيْهِ are found in a single phrase. For example,

الرَّجُلِ	بَيْتِ	بَابُ	the door of the man's house
مُضَافٌ إِلَيْهِ	مُضَافٌ إِلَيْهِ وَمُضَافٌ	مُضَافٌ	

2. If the مُضَافٌ has a صِفَةٌ, then it should come immediately after the مُضَافٌ إِلَيْهِ with an ال and should have the same إِعْرَابٌ as that of the مُضَافٌ. For example,

الْجَدِيدُ	الْبَيْتِ	بَابُ	the new door of the house
صِفَةُ الْمُضَافِ	مُضَافٌ إِلَيْهِ	مُضَافٌ	

3. If the مُضَافٌ إِلَيْهِ has a صِفَةٌ, then it should come immediately after the مُضَافٌ إِلَيْهِ, and should correspond to it (مُضَافٌ إِلَيْهِ) in the four aspects mentioned earlier. For example,

3. <u>اَلْمُرَكَّبُ الْإِشَارِيُّ</u> – **Demonstrative phrase:** It is a phrase in which one اِسْمٌ (اِسْمُ الْإِشَارَةِ) points towards another اِسْمٌ (مُشَارٌ إِلَيْهِ).

- The مُشَارٌ إِلَيْهِ must have an ال.

	الرَّجُلُ	هَذَا	This man
e.g.	مُشَارٌ إِلَيْهِ	اِسْمُ الْإِشَارَةِ	

Note: If the مُشَارٌ إِلَيْهِ does not have an ال, it would be a complete sentence.

	رَجُلٌ	هَذَا	This is a man.
e.g.	خَبَرٌ + مُبْتَدَأٌ	= جُمْلَةٌ اِسْمِيَّةٌ	

4. <u>اَلْمُرَكَّبُ الْبِنَائِيُّ/ اَلْمُرَكَّبُ الْعَدَدِيُّ</u> – **Numerical phrase:** It is a phrase in which two numerals are joined to form a single word (number).

- A حَرْفٌ originally linked the two.

  e.g. أَحَدَ عَشَرَ (eleven)   It was originally أَحَدٌ وَعَشْرٌ.

- This phrase is found only in numbers 11-19.

  e.g. (19) تِسْعَ عَشَرَ ... ,(13) ثَلَاثَ عَشَرَ, (12) اِثْنَا عَشَرَ, (11) أَحَدَ عَشَرَ

- Both parts of this phrase will always be مَفْتُوحٌ except the number 12 (إِثْنَا عَشَرَ).

		e.g.
(حَالَةُ الرَّفْعِ) جَاءَ أَحَدَ عَشَرَ رَجُلًا	(حَالَةُ النَّصْبِ) رَأَيْتُ أَحَدَ عَشَرَ رَجُلًا	
Eleven men came.	I saw eleven men.	

(حَالَةُ الْجَرِّ) مَرَرْتُ بِأَحَدَ عَشَرَ رَجُلًا

I passed by eleven men.

- As for number 12, its second part is always مَفْتُوحٌ while the first part changes. Thus, in حَالَةُ الرَّفْعِ, it is written as إِثْنَا عَشَرَ, with an ا at the end of the first part. However, in حَالَةُ النَّصْبِ and حَالَةُ الْجَرِّ, the first part is given a ي in place of the ا (إِثْنَيْ عَشَرَ).

		e.g.
(حَالَةُ الرَّفْعِ) جَاءَ إِثْنَا عَشَرَ رَجُلًا	(حَالَةُ النَّصْبِ) رَأَيْتُ إِثْنَيْ عَشَرَ رَجُلًا	
Twelve men came.	I saw twelve men.	

(حَالَةُ الْجَرِّ) مَرَرْتُ بِاِثْنَيْ عَشَرَ رَجُلًا

I passed by twelve men.

5. <u>الْمُرَكَّبُ مَنْعُ الصَّرْفِ</u> – **Indeclinable phrase:** It is a phrase in which two words are joined to form a single word.

- The first part of this phrase is always مَفْتُوحٌ.
- The second part changes according to the عَامِلٌ.

Examples:

1. حَضَرَمَوْتُ is the name of a region in Yemen. It is composed of two words حَضَرَ and مَوْتٌ. حَضَرَ is a فِعْلٌ, which means "he/it was present" and مَوْتٌ is an إِسْمٌ, which means "death." Thus, literally, حَضَرَمَوْتُ means "[a place where] death was present."

2. بَعْلَبَكُّ is a city in Lebanon. It is composed of two words بَعْلٌ and بَكٌّ. بَعْلٌ was the name of an idol and بَكٌّ was the name of a king.

<u>Note:</u> The above mentioned various types of phrases/incomplete sentences form part of a complete sentence.

Example 1	الْأَمِيْنُ	التَّاجِرُ	رَبِحَ	The trustworthy/honest trader gained profit.

مَوْصُوْفٌ + صِفَةٌ

جُمْلَةٌ فِعْلِيَّةٌ خَبَرِيَّةٌ = فَاعِلٌ + فِعْلٌ

11

Example 2

مَرْفُوعٌ   فَاعِلٍ   كُلُّ

مَنْصُوبٌ   مَفْعُولٍ   كُلُّ   وَ

Every *faa'il* is *marfoo'* and every *maf'ool* is *mansoob*.

مُضَافٌ + مُضَافٌ إِلَيْهِ

مُبْتَدَأٌ   +   خَبَرٌ   =   جُمْلَةٌ اِسْمِيَّةٌ خَبَرِيَّةٌ

Example 3

الْكِتَابَ   هٰذَا   اِشْتَرَيْتُ

I bought this book.

اِسْمُ الْإِشَارَةِ + مُشَارٌ إِلَيْهِ

جُمْلَةٌ فِعْلِيَّةٌ خَبَرِيَّةٌ   =   مَفْعُولٌ   +   فِعْلٌ مَعَ فَاعِلِهِ

Example 4

أَرْبَعَةَ عَشَرَ رَجُلًا   جَاءَ

Fourteen men came.

جُمْلَةٌ فِعْلِيَّةٌ خَبَرِيَّةٌ   =   فَاعِلٌ   +   فِعْلٌ

Example 5

بَعْلَبَكُّ   هٰذِهِ

This is Ba'labakk.

جُمْلَةٌ اِسْمِيَّةٌ خَبَرِيَّةٌ   =   خَبَرٌ   +   مُبْتَدَأٌ

EXERCISES

1. Translate, fill in the إِعْرَابٌ and analyze the following phrases.

i.	سيارة الرجل	v.	الوردة الجميلة
ii.	أربع عشر	vi.	قلم رخيص
iii.	باب فصل المدرسة	vii.	معديكرب
iv.	قلم الرجل الطويل	viii.	ذلك الكتاب

2. What is the difference between the following phrases/sentences?

i.	غُلَامٌ عَاقِلٌ	and	غُلَامُ عَاقِلٍ
ii.	هذه تفاحة	and	هذه التفاحة
iii.	نافذة السيارة الكبيرةُ	and	نافذة السيارة الكبيرةِ
iv.	الثوب نظيفٌ	and	الثوب النظيف

3. Correct the following and state the reason(s).

i.	وَلَدٌ القبيحٌ	iii.	المعلمُ المدرسةِ
ii.	الرجلان الطويل	iv.	ثمانيةُ عَشَرٍ

4. Translate, fill in the إِعْرَابٌ and analyze the following.

i.	باب فضل قيام ليلة القدر

<u>Section 1.4.4</u>

<u>Additional notes about جُمْلَةٌ اِسْمِيَّةٌ</u>

1. Sometimes, the خَبَرٌ is not mentioned, in which case it will be regarded as hidden (مُقَدَّرٌ).[7]

    e.g.   أَلْإِمَامُ فِي الْمَسْجِدِ   The Imam is in the mosque.

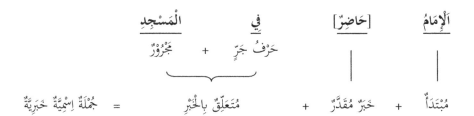

الْمَسْجِدِ	فِي	[حَاضِرٌ]	اَلْإِمَامُ
مَجْرُورٌ +	حَرْفُ جَرٍّ		
جُمْلَةٌ اِسْمِيَّةٌ خَبَرِيَّةٌ =	مُتَعَلِّقٌ بِالْخَبَرِ	خَبَرٌ مُقَدَّرٌ +	مُبْتَدَأٌ +

2. The خَبَرٌ can be a complete sentence.

    Example 1:   زَيْدٌ أَبُوهُ عَالِمٌ   Zayd's father is knowledgeable.

عَالِمٌ	أَبُوهُ	زَيْدٌ
	مُضَافٌ + مُضَافٌ إِلَيْهِ	
جُمْلَةٌ اِسْمِيَّةٌ خَبَرِيَّةٌ =	خَبَرٌ + مُبْتَدَأٌ	
جُمْلَةٌ اِسْمِيَّةٌ خَبَرِيَّةٌ =	خَبَرٌ	مُبْتَدَأٌ +

    Example 2:   زَيْدٌ أَكَلَ الطَّعَامَ   Zayd ate the food.

الطَّعَامَ	أَكَلَ	زَيْدٌ
جُمْلَةٌ فِعْلِيَّةٌ خَبَرِيَّةٌ =	مَفْعُولٌ + فِعْلٌ مَعَ فَاعِلِهِ	
جُمْلَةٌ اِسْمِيَّةٌ خَبَرِيَّةٌ =	خَبَرٌ	مُبْتَدَأٌ +

EXERCISE

1. Translate, fill in the إِعْرَابٌ and analyze the following sentences.

    ii. الثور يحرث الأرض   i. القلم في الفصل

---

[7] However, generally, to simplify matters, the مُتَعَلِّقٌ is taken to be the خَبَرٌ. See Mawlana Hasan Dockrat, *A Simplified Arabic Grammar* (Azaadvillle: Madrasa Arabia Islamia, 2003), 37.

Summary

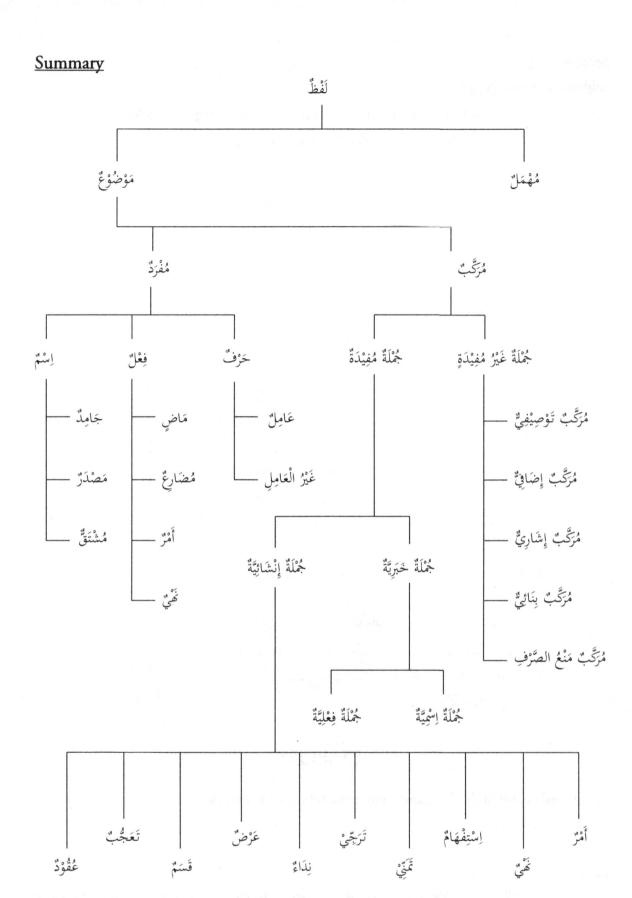

Section 1.5

عَلَامَاتُ الْاِسْمِ – Signs of an *ism*:

1.	It is preceded by an ال.	e.g.	اَلرَّجُلُ	the man
2.	It accepts جَرٌّ.	e.g.	فِيْ بَيْتِ زَيْدِنِ الْجَدِيْدِ	in Zayd's new house
3.	There is تَنْوِيْنٌ on the last letter.	e.g.	رَجُلٌ	a man
4.	It ends with a round ة.	e.g.	كَلِمَةٌ	a word
5.	It is a dual (تَثْنِيَةٌ).[8]	e.g.	رَجُلَانِ	two men
6.	It is a plural (جَمْعٌ).	e.g.	رِجَالٌ	men
7.	It is a (فَاعِلٌ or مُبْتَدَأٌ) مُسْنَدٌ إِلَيْهِ.	e.g.	اَلرَّجُلُ قَوِيٌّ	The man is strong.
		e.g.	جَلَسَ زَيْدٌ	Zayd sat.
8.	It is مُضَافٌ.	e.g.	كِتَابُ زَيْدٍ	book of Zayd
9.	It is مَوْصُوْفٌ.	e.g.	رَجُلٌ طَوِيْلٌ	tall man
10.	It is مُنَادًى.	e.g.	يَا رَجُلُ	O man!
11.	It is مُصَغَّرٌ.	e.g.	رُجَيْلٌ	a little man
12.	It is مَنْسُوْبٌ.	e.g.	مَكِّيٌّ	a Makkan

عَلَامَاتُ الْفِعْلِ – Signs of a *fi'l*:

1.	It is preceded by قَدْ.	e.g.	قَدْ خَرَجَ	He has gone out.
2.	It is preceded by سَ.	e.g.	سَيَخْرُجُ	He will soon go out.
3.	It is preceded by سَوْفَ.	e.g.	سَوْفَ يَخْرُجُ	He will go out after a while.
4.	It is preceded by حَرْفُ جَزْمٍ.	e.g.	لَمْ يَخْرُجْ	He did not go out.
5.	It is preceded by حَرْفُ نَصْبٍ.	e.g.	لَنْ يَخْرُجَ	He will never go out.
6.	It has a hidden ضَمِيْرٌ.	e.g.	خَرَجَ	He went out.
7.	It is an imperative (أَمْرٌ).	e.g.	اُخْرُجْ	Go out.
8.	It is a prohibitive (نَهْيٌ).	e.g.	لَا تَخْرُجْ	Do not go out.
9.	It has *taa saakin* (ت) at the end.	e.g.	أَكَلَتْ	She ate.

عَلَامَةُ الْحَرْفِ – Sign of a particle:

That word which has no sign of an اِسْمٌ or a فِعْلٌ is a particle (a particle has no sign of its own).

---

[8] A فِعْلٌ is said to be dual or plural with respect to its doer (فَاعِلٌ). The action is one. Thus, duality and plurality are signs of an اِسْمٌ and not a فِعْلٌ.

Section 1.5.1
General notes

1. The indefiniteness of an اِسْمٌ is indicated by a تَنْوِينٌ. Such an اِسْمٌ is called نَكِرَةٌ.

   e.g.   بَيْتٌ   a house (any house)

2. The definiteness of an اِسْمٌ is indicated by an ال. Such an اِسْمٌ is called مَعْرِفَةٌ.

   e.g.   اَلْبَيْتُ   the house (a specific house)

3. An اِسْمٌ can never have a تَنْوِينٌ and an ال at the same time.

   e.g.   اَلْبَيْتٌ   is incorrect.

4. When the last letter of a word and the first letter of the following word have سُكُونٌ (ـْ), it is called اِجْتِمَاعُ السَّاكِنَيْنِ (the meeting of two *sukoons*). In this case, the first *sukoon* is generally changed to a *kasrah*.

   e.g.   ضَرَبَتِ الْبِنْتُ will become ضَرَبَتْ الْبِنْتُ. The هَمْزَةُ الْوَصْلِ before the ل is not pronounced.

   In some cases, the first *sukoon* is changed to a *fathah*.

   e.g.   مِنَ الْيَابَانِ (from Japan) becomes مِنْ الْيَابَانِ.

   In some cases, the first *sukoon* is changed to *dammah*.

   e.g.   فَهِمْتُمُ الدَّرْسَ (you understood the lesson) becomes فَهِمْتُمْ الدَّرْسَ.

5. When an ال appears before an اِسْمٌ which begins with a letter from اَلْحُرُوفُ الشَّمْسِيَّةُ (sun letters) then the ل of ال must not be pronounced. The ل of ال does not receive a *sukoon*. Instead the حَرْفٌ شَمْسِيٌّ receives a *tashdeed*.

   e.g.   اَلشَّجَرَةُ   the tree   اَلشَّمْسُ   the sun

   ت ث د ذ ر ز س ش ص ض ط ظ ل ن = اَلْحُرُوفُ الشَّمْسِيَّةُ

6. The remaining letters are known as اَلْحُرُوفُ الْقَمَرِيَّةُ (moon letters). In these, the ل of ال receives a *sukoon* and is pronounced. The حَرْفٌ قَمَرِيٌّ does not receive a *tashdeed*.

   e.g.   اَلْقَلَمُ   the pen   اَلْقَمَرُ   the moon

7. Generally, an اِسْمٌ ending with a round ة (اَلتَّاءُ الْمَرْبُوطَةُ) is a feminine (مُؤَنَّثٌ).

   e.g.   سَبُّورَةٌ   blackboard

8. The صِفَةٌ – اِسْمُ الْإِشَارَةِ – فِعْلٌ – اَلْاِسْمُ الْمَوْصُولُ – خَبَرٌ etc. of a غَيْرُ الْعَاقِلِ (non-human) plural is generally وَاحِدٌ مُؤَنَّثٌ.

e.g.	أَصْنَامٌ كَثِيرَةٌ	many idols	اَلْأَصْنَامُ لَا تَنْفَعُ	The idols do not benefit.
	هٰذِهِ الْأَصْنَامُ	these idols	اَلْكِلَابُ الْحَارِسَةُ جَالِسَةٌ	The guard dogs are sitting.
			كَانَتِ الْبُيُوتُ كَثِيرَةً	The houses were many.

9. When writing an اِسْمٌ ending with two *fathahs* (ـً), an *alif* (ا) must be added at the end.

    e.g.   زَيْدًا

    However, If there is a round ة (اَلتَّاءُ الْمَرْبُوطَةُ) at the end of such a word, *alif* should not be added.

    e.g.   رِسَالَةً

18

Section 1.6
اَلضَّمَائِرُ – Personal pronouns

<u>Definition:</u> ضَمَائِر (singular: ضَمِيرٌ) are those words which are used in place of names and refer to the speaker (مُتَكَلِّمٌ) or the second person (حَاضِرٌ) or the third person (غَائِبٌ).

Table 1.1

اَلضَّمَائِرُ – Personal pronouns

Unattached form (مُنْفَصِلٌ)		Attached form (مُتَّصِلٌ)			
هُوَ	He (one male), it	هُ	his, its, him	وَاحِدٌ مُذَكَّرٌ غَائِبٌ (Singular)	3rd Person Masculine
هُمَا	They (two males)	هُمَا	their, them	تَثْنِيَةٌ مُذَكَّرٌ غَائِبٌ (Dual)	
هُمْ	They (many males)	هُمْ	their, them	جَمْعٌ مُذَكَّرٌ غَائِبٌ (Plural)	
هِيَ	She (one female), it	هَا	her, its	وَاحِدٌ مُؤَنَّثٌ غَائِبٌ (Singular)	3rd Person Feminine
هُمَا	They (two females)	هُمَا	their, them	تَثْنِيَةٌ مُؤَنَّثٌ غَائِبٌ (Dual)	
هُنَّ	They (many females)	هُنَّ	their, them	جَمْعٌ مُؤَنَّثٌ غَائِبٌ (Plural)	
أَنْتَ	You (one male)	كَ	your	وَاحِدٌ مُذَكَّرٌ حَاضِرٌ (Singular)	2nd Person Masculine
أَنْتُمَا	You (two males)	كُمَا	your	تَثْنِيَةٌ مُذَكَّرٌ حَاضِرٌ (Dual)	
أَنْتُمْ	You (many males)	كُمْ	your	جَمْعٌ مُذَكَّرٌ حَاضِرٌ (Plural)	
أَنْتِ	You (one female)	كِ	your	وَاحِدٌ مُؤَنَّثٌ حَاضِرٌ (Singular)	2nd Person Feminine
أَنْتُمَا	You (two females)	كُمَا	your	تَثْنِيَةٌ مُؤَنَّثٌ حَاضِرٌ (Dual)	
أَنْتُنَّ	You (many females)	كُنَّ	your	جَمْعٌ مُؤَنَّثٌ حَاضِرٌ (Plural)	
أَنَا	I (one male or female)	ـِي، نِي[9]	my, mine, me	وَاحِدٌ مُتَكَلِّمٌ (مُذَكَّرٌ وَمُؤَنَّثٌ) (Singular)	1st Person Masc. & Fem.
نَحْنُ	We (many males or females)	نَا	our	(مُذَكَّرٌ وَمُؤَنَّثٌ) تَثْنِيَةٌ وَجَمْعٌ مُتَكَلِّمٌ (Dual & Plural)	

In the unattached form, these *dameers* can appear as *mubtada*, *faa'il*, etc. In the attached form, they can appear as *maf'ool* or *mudaaf ilayhi*. For more details, see section 2.4.1.

e.g. هُوَ زَيْدٌ   He is Zayd.   قَلَمُكَ   your pen

أَنَا طَالِبٌ   I am a student.   نَصَرْتُهَا   I helped her.

---

[9] Sometimes, a ن (نُونُ الْوِقَايَةِ) is added before the ضَمِيرٌ يَاء to protect an *i'raab* such as in ضَرَبَنِي, which would otherwise be incorrectly read as ضَرَبِي (the لَامُ الْكَلِمَةِ of اَلْفِعْلُ الْمَاضِى is مَبْنِيٌّ عَلَى الْفَتْحِ).

Section 1.7[10]
اَلْحُرُوفُ الْجَارَّةُ – Prepositions

Effect: A حَرْفُ جَرٍّ gives a جَرّ to the اِسْم it acts upon which is then known as مَجْرُورٌ.

Table 1.2
اَلْحُرُوفُ الْجَارَّةُ – Prepositions

	حَرْفُ جَرٍّ	Meaning		Example
1.	بِ	with	كَتَبْتُ بِالْقَلَمِ	I wrote with the pen.
2.	تَ	by (for oath)	تَاللهِ	By Allah!
3.	كَ	like	زَيْدٌ كَالْأَسَدِ	Zayd is like a lion.
4.	لِ	for	اَلْحَمْدُ للهِ	All praise is for Allah.
5.	وَ	by (oath)	وَاللهِ	By Allah!
6.	مُنْذُ	since	مَا رَأَيْتُهُ مُنْذُ يَوْمِ الْأَحَدِ	I have not seen him since Sunday.
7.	مُذْ	since/for	مَا رَأَيْتُهُ مُذْ أَرْبَعَةِ أَيَّامٍ	I have not see him for four days.
8.	خَلَا	besides, except	جَاءَ النَّاسُ خَلَا زَيْدٍ	The people came except Zayd.
9.	رُبَّ	many a…	رُبَّ عَالِمٍ يَعْمَلُ بِعِلْمِهِ	Many a learned person acts on his knowledge.
10.	حَاشَا	besides, except	جَاءَ النَّاسُ حَاشَا زَيْدٍ	The people came except Zayd.
11.	مِنْ	from	رَجَعْتُ مِنَ السَّفَرِ	I returned from the journey.
12.	عَدَا	besides, except	جَاءَ النَّاسُ عَدَا زَيْدٍ	The people came except Zayd.
13.	فِي	in, regarding	زَيْدٌ فِي الْبَيْتِ	Zayd is in the house.
14.	عَنْ	regarding	سَأَلَ الطَّبِيْبُ عَنِ الْمَرِيْضِ	The doctor asked about the patient.
15.	عَلَى	on	اَلثَّوْبُ عَلَى الْكُرْسِيِّ	The cloth/clothes is/are on the chair.
16.	حَتَّى	up to, until	نِمْتُ حَتَّى الصُّبْحِ	I slept till dawn.
17.	إِلَى	up to, towards	سَافَرْتُ إِلَى الْمَدِيْنَةِ	I travelled to Madinah.

Example 1:   اَلنَّحْوُ فِي الْكَلَامِ كَالْمِلْحِ فِي الطَّعَامِ   Grammar in speech is like salt in food.

---

[10] For more examples and exercises, please refer to *al-Nahw al-Wadih, Ibtida'iyyah*, vol. 1, 76-81.

Example 2 with sentence analysis:

كَتَبْتُ   بِالْقَلَمِ   I wrote with the pen.

حَرْفُ جَرٍّ + مَجْرُورٌ

فِعْلٌ + فَاعِلٌ + مُتَعَلِّقٌ بِالْفِعْلِ = جُمْلَةٌ فِعْلِيَّةٌ خَبَرِيَّةٌ

<u>Note:</u> Together, the حَرْفُ جَرٍّ and مَجْرُورٌ are known as مُتَعَلِّقٌ (connected) of the خَبَر in جُمْلَةٌ اِسْمِيَّةٌ (there is more detail to this, and will be discussed later), and of the فِعْلٌ in جُمْلَةٌ فِعْلِيَّةٌ.

EXERCISE

1. Translate, fill in the *i'raab* and analyze the following sentences.

    iii. الكتب على المنضدة   i. المسجد قريب من بيت زيد

    iv. زينب جالسة على الكرسي فى الحجرة   ii. نزل المطر من السماء

Section 1.8[11]

اَلْحُرُوفُ الْمُشَبَّهَةُ بِالْفِعْلِ (also called إِنَّ وَأَخَوَاتُهَا) – Particles that resemble a *fi'l*

- These are called اَلْحُرُوفُ الْمُشَبَّهَةُ بِالْفِعْلِ because like اَلْفِعْلُ الْمُتَعَدِّيْ, they also govern two words.
- These حُرُوفٌ appear before a مُبْتَدَأ and a خَبَر (جُمْلَةٌ اِسْمِيَّةٌ).

<u>Effect:</u> Such a particle causes the مُبْتَدَأ to be in a state of نَصْبٌ which is then known as اِسْمُ إِنَّ (or اِسْمُ أَنَّ and so on) and causes the خَبَر to be in a state of رَفْعٌ which is then known as خَبَرُ إِنَّ (or خَبَرُ أَنَّ and so on).

Table 1.3
اَلْحُرُوفُ الْمُشَبَّهَةُ بِالْفِعْلِ – Particles that resemble a *fi'l*

		Meaning	Example	
1.	إِنَّ	certainly, verily, indeed	إِنَّ اللهَ عَلِيْمٌ	Verily Allah is All-Knowing.
2.	أَنَّ	that	أَعْرِفُ أَنَّ الْاِمْتِحَانَ قَرِيْبٌ	I know that the examination is near.
3.	كَأَنَّ	as if	كَأَنَّ الْبَيْتَ جَدِيْدٌ	It is as if the house is new.
4.	لٰكِنَّ	but, however	اَلْبَيْتُ جَدِيْدٌ لٰكِنَّ الْأَثَاثَ قَدِيْمٌ	The house is new but the furniture is old.
5.	لَيْتَ	if only, I wish	لَيْتَ الشَّبَابَ عَائِدٌ	I wish youth would return.
6.	لَعَلَّ	maybe, hopefully, perhaps	لَعَلَّ الْاِمْتِحَانَ سَهْلٌ	Hopefully, the examination will be easy.

Sentence Analysis:

عَلِيْمٌ	اللهَ	إِنَّ	Indeed, Allah is All-Knowing.
اَلْحَرْفُ الْمُشَبَّهُ بِالْفِعْلِ	اِسْمُ إِنَّ	خَبَرُ إِنَّ	

Notes:

1. Difference between إِنَّ and أَنَّ:

   a. إِنَّ is generally used at the beginning of a sentence.

   أَنَّ is generally used in the middle of a sentence.

---

[11] For more examples and exercises, please refer to *al-Nahw al-Wadih, Ibtida'iyyah*, vol. 1, 69-75.

b. Sometimes, إِنَّ appears in the middle of a sentence. This happens in the following two cases:

    i. When it is used after a word with root letters ق – و – ل.

        e.g.   يَقُوْلُ إِنَّهَا بَقَرَةٌ صَفْرَاءُ   He says, indeed, it is a yellow cow.

    ii. When it is at the beginning of a صِلَةٌ.[12]

        e.g.   زُرْتُ الَّذِيْ إِنِّيْ أَحْتَرِمُهُ   I visited the one whom I respect.

2. The خَبَرٌ can be a complete sentence.

    Example 1:   إِنَّ زَيْدًا أُمُّهُ صَالِحَةٌ   Indeed, Zayd's mother is pious.

    Example 2:   إِنَّ زَيْدًا أَكَلَ الطَّعَامَ   Indeed, Zayd ate the food.

3. If the خَبَرٌ is (جَارٌّ وَمَجْرُوْرٌ), then the خَبَرٌ will appear first and the اِسْمٌ second.

    e.g.   إِنَّ إِلَيْنَا إِيَابَهُمْ   Indeed, to us is their return.

---

[12] صِلَةٌ will be discussed in Section 2.4.2.

4. When مَا الْكَافَّةُ is joined to any of these حُرُوفٌ, their effect is cancelled.

e.g.   إِنَّمَا إِلَهُكُمْ إِلَهٌ وَّاحِدٌ   Your god is only one god.

Note: In this example, the meaning has also changed to "only."

5. إِنَّ by itself conveys emphasis. Sometimes, لَامُ التَّأْكِيدِ can be added before the خَبَرٌ to convey even more emphasis.

e.g.   إِنَّكَ لَرَسُوْلُ اللهِ   Indeed, you are the messenger of Allah.

إِنِّيْ لَأَعْرِفُ أَخَاكَ   Indeed, I know your brother.

EXCERISE

1. Translate, fill in the *i'raab*, and analyze the following sentences.

i. لعل المريض نائم   iv. كأن القمر مصباح

ii. اعلم أن زيدا عاقل   v. ليت القمر طالع

iii. إن رجلا دخل البيت   vi. إن علينا بيانه

24

Section 1.9[13]
اَلْأَفْعَالُ النَّاقِصَةُ also called (كَانَ وَأَخَوَاتُهَا) – Auxiliary (defective) *fi'ls*

- فِعْلٌ نَاقِصٌ is called نَاقِصٌ (incomplete/defective) because even though it is a فِعْلٌ لَازِمٌ, it needs two *ma'mools* (مَعْمُولَيْنِ). The sentence remains incomplete with one مَعْمُولٌ.

  e.g.   كَانَ زَيْدٌ   Zayd was (the sentence remains incomplete).

- These أَفْعَال enter upon a مُبْتَدَأٌ and a خَبَرٌ.

Effect: They give رَفْعٌ to the مُبْتَدَأٌ which is then known as اِسْمُ كَانَ (or اِسْمُ صَارَ and so on) and نَصْبٌ to the خَبَرٌ which is then known as خَبَرُ كَانَ (or خَبَرُ صَارَ and so on).

Table 1.4

فِعْلٌ نَاقِصٌ	Meaning	Example	
1. كَانَ	was	كَانَ الْبَيْتُ نَظِيْفًا	The house was clean.
2. صَارَ	became	صَارَ الرَّجُلُ غَنِيًّا	The man became wealthy.
3. أَصْبَحَ	happen in the morning OR became	أَصْبَحَ زَيْدٌ مَرِيْضًا أَصْبَحَ زَيْدٌ غَنِيًّا	Zayd became ill in the morning. Zayd became rich.
4. أَمْسَى	happen in the evening, became	أَمْسَى الْعَامِلُ مُتْعَبًا	The worker became tired in the evening.
5. أَضْحَى	happen at midmorning, became	أَضْحَى الْغَمَامُ كَثِيْفًا	The clouds became dense at mid morning.
6. ظَلَّ	happen during the day, became	ظَلَّ الْمَطَرُ نَازِلًا	It rained the whole day.
7. بَاتَ	happen during the night, became	بَاتَ زَيْدٌ نَائِمًا	Zayd passed the night sleeping.
8. مَا دَامَ	as long as	اِجْلِسْ مَا دَامَ زَيْدٌ جَالِسًا	Sit as long as Zayd is sitting.
9. مَا زَالَ	always, continuously	مَا زَالَ زَيْدٌ مَرِيْضًا	Zayd was continuously sick.
10. مَا بَرِحَ	always, continuously	مَا بَرِحَ زَيْدٌ صَائِمًا	Zayd was always fasting.
11. مَا فَتِئَ	always, continuously	مَا فَتِئَ زَيْدٌ نَشِيْطًا	Zayd was always active.
12. مَا انْفَكَّ	always, continuously	مَا انْفَكَّ التَّاجِرُ صَادِقًا	The trader was always truthful.
13. لَيْسَ	no, not	لَيْسَ الْخَادِمُ قَوِيًّا	The servant is not strong.

---

[13] For more examples and exercises, please refer to *al-Nahw al-Wadih, Ibtida'iyyah*, vol. 1, 62-68 & vol. 2, 151-155.

Sentence Analysis:

نَظِيْفًا	الْبَيْتُ	كَانَ	The house was clean.
خَبَرُ كَانَ	اِسْمُ كَانَ	فِعْلٌ نَاقِصٌ	

Notes:

1. When كَانَ is used with مُضَارِعٌ, it gives the meaning of past continuous or past habitual.

   e.g.   كَانَ زَيْدٌ يَكْتُبُ   Zayd was writing/Zayd used to write.

   <u>Note:</u> Here, the خَبَر of كَانَ is a جُمْلَةٌ فِعْلِيَّةٌ. Also, note the two ways it is translated above.

2. كَانَ – صَارَ – أَصْبَحَ – أَمْسَى – أَضْحَى – ظَلَّ – بَاتَ can be used in مُضَارِعٌ, أَمْرٌ and نَهْيٌ as well.

3. مَا زَالَ – مَا بَرِحَ – مَا فَتِئَ – مَا انْفَكَّ can be used in مُضَارِعٌ but not in أَمْرٌ.

4. مَا دَامَ and لَيْسَ have a past tense only (no مُضَارِعٌ or أَمْرٌ).

5. مَا دَامَ must be preceded by another sentence.

6. The خَبَر of لَيْسَ is sometimes prefixed with a بِ.

   e.g.   أَلَيْسَ اللهُ بِأَحْكَمِ الْحَاكِمِيْنَ   Is Allah not the greatest of rulers/best of judges?

7. If the خَبَر is (جَارٌّ وَمَجْرُورٌ), then the خَبَر will appear first and the مُبْتَدَأٌ second.

   e.g.

سَحَابٌ	فِي السَّمَاءِ	كَانَ	There were clouds in the sky.
فِعْلٌ نَاقِصٌ	خَبَرُ كَانَ (مُقَدَّمٌ)	اِسْمُ كَانَ (مُؤَخَّرٌ)	

EXERCISE

1. Translate, fill in the i'raab, and analyze the following sentences.

v.	صار الكبش سمينا	i.	ليس العامل نشيطا
vi.	لا يزال لسانك رطبا من ذكر الله	ii.	كان منامه مناما صادقا
vii.	يصبح المداد جافا	iii.	أمسى الغني فقيرا
		iv.	نويت الاعتكاف ما دمت في المسجد

26

CHAPTER 2

اَلْمُعْرَبُ وَالْمَبْنِيُّ – Declinable and indeclinable words

Words are of two types with respect to changes that occur at their ends. If the end remains the same in all conditions, the word is called مَبْنِيٌّ; and if it does change, the word is called مُعْرَبٌ.

Section 2.1[14]

أَنْوَاعُ الْبِنَاءِ: The conditions or states (أَحْوَالٌ) which remain unchanged at the end of مَبْنِيٌّ words are four: سُكُوْنٌ, فَتْحٌ, كَسْرٌ and ضَمٌّ. These are called أَنْوَاعُ الْبِنَاءِ.

أَنْوَاعُ الْإِعْرَابِ: Those conditions or states (أَحْوَالٌ) which occur at the end of مُعْرَبٌ words are four: رَفْعٌ, نَصْبٌ, جَرٌّ, and جَزْمٌ. These are called أَنْوَاعُ الْإِعْرَابِ (اَلْإِعْرَابُ for short). These changes are brought about at the end of a مُعْرَبٌ word in accordance with the requirement of the عَامِلٌ (governing word).

عَلَامَاتُ الْإِعْرَابِ – Signs of i'raab

The i'raab shows in various ways. These are called عَلَامَاتُ الْإِعْرَابِ (signs of i'raab). The two common ones are as follows:

1. اَلْإِعْرَابُ بِالْحَرَكَةِ: These are the basic signs and are the most common. I'raab is shown by means of a حَرَكَةٌ i.e. ضَمَّةٌ or فَتْحَةٌ or كَسْرَةٌ or سُكُوْنٌ (which is the absence of a حَرَكَةٌ).

   e.g.   رَجُلٌ   رَجُلًا   رَجُلٍ   لَمْ يَضْرِبْ

2. اَلْإِعْرَابُ بِالْحُرُوفِ: Sometimes, the i'raab is shown by means of any of the حُرُوفُ عِلَّةٍ i.e. و or ا or ي.

   e.g.   أَبُوْكَ   أَبَاكَ   أَبِيْكَ

---

[14] This section is based upon the discussion in *al-Nahw al-Wadih*. See *al-Nahw al-Wadih, Ibdtida'iyyah*, vol. 2, 7-18.

حَالَاتُ الْمُعْرَب – States of *mu'rab*

As mentioned above, the conditions or states that occur at the end of مُعْرَب words are four. Below, we look at them in more detail.

1. حَالَةُ الرَّفْع is the condition in which a ضَمَّةٌ or its substitute such as (و) حَرْفُ عِلَّةٍ appears at the end of a word. Such a word is said to be مَرْفُوعٌ.

   e.g. أَبُو خَالِدٍ   أَخُوكَ   أَخٌ

2. حَالَةُ النَّصْب is the condition in which a فَتْحَةٌ or its substitute such as (ا) حَرْفُ عِلَّةٍ appears at the end of a word. Such a word is said to be مَنْصُوبٌ.

   e.g. أَبَا خَالِدٍ   أَخَاكَ   أَخًا

3. حَالَةُ الْجَرِّ is the condition in which a كَسْرَةٌ or its substitute such as (ي) حَرْفُ عِلَّةٍ appears at the end of a word. Such a word is said to be مَجْرُورٌ.

   e.g. أَبِي خَالِدٍ   أَخِيكَ   أَخٍ

4. حَالَةُ الْجَزْم is the condition in which a سُكُونٌ appears at the end of a word or its substitute (ن in the case of فِعْلٌ مُضَارِعٌ) is dropped from the end. Such a word is said to be مَجْزُومٌ.

   e.g. لَمْ يَضْرِبُوا   لَمْ يَضْرِبْ

Note: It should be remembered that *fi'l*s can only be in the state of رَفْعٌ, نَصْبٌ or جَزْمٌ, while *ism*s can only be in a state of رَفْعٌ, نَصْبٌ, or جَرٌّ.

The difference between كَسْرٌ – فَتْحٌ – ضَمٌّ and كَسْرَةٌ – فَتْحَةٌ – ضَمَّةٌ

- The words كَسْرٌ – فَتْحٌ – ضَمٌّ are used to describe the states at the end of a مَبْنِيّ , e.g. ضَرَبَ has a فَتْحٌ at the end. It is مَبْنِيٌّ عَلَى الْفَتْحِ.

- The words كَسْرَةٌ – فَتْحَةٌ – ضَمَّةٌ are used for all other places where (ـُ), (ـَ) and (ـِ) appear.

In other words, (ـُ), (ـَ) and (ـِ) are normally called كَسْرَةٌ – فَتْحَةٌ – ضَمَّةٌ, respectively, wherever they occur except when one needs to precisely point out the end of a مَبْنِيّ word. Thus, one would say ضَرَبَ has a فَتْحَةٌ on (ض), a فَتْحَةٌ on (ر), and a فَتْحَةٌ on (ب), but one must say (ضَرَبَ) is مَبْنِيٌّ عَلَى الْفَتْحِ.

28

Section 2.2

اَلْمَبْنِيُّ – The indeclinable word

As mentioned earlier, a مَبْنِيٌّ is a word whose end remains unchanged in all conditions i.e. irrespective of the requirement of the عَامِلٌ governing it.

مَرَرْتُ بِهٰذَا	رَأَيْتُ هٰذَا	جَاءَ هٰذَا	e.g.
I passed by this.	I saw this.	This came.	

<u>Note:</u> The حَرَكَةٌ at the end of هٰذَا remains constant and does not change according to the عَامِلٌ requirement.

<u>Types of</u> مَبْنِيٌّ:

1. All Particles (حُرُوفٌ) *

2. اَلْفِعْلُ الْمَاضِيْ *

3. اَلْأَمْرُ الْحَاضِرُ الْمَعْرُوْفُ *

4. Those *seeghahs* of فِعْلٌ مُضَارِعٌ that are جَمْعُ مُؤَنَّثٍ (حَاضِرٌ and غَائِبٌ) or have نُوْنُ التَّأْكِيْدِ (ثَقِيْلَةٌ and خَفِيْفَةٌ).

5. Amongst *isms*, those whose ends remain constant are called غَيْرُ الْمُتَمَكِّنِ i.e. *isms* which do not give place to changes. These *isms* are مَبْنِيٌّ and are recognized by their resemblance with any one of the three types of الْمَبْنِيُّ الْأَصْلُ words (حُرُوْفٌ or الْفِعْلُ الْمَاضِى or اَلْأَمْرُ الْحَاضِرُ الْمَعْرُوْفُ). This resemblance can be in any one of the following ways:

   a. Resemblance in meaning. For example, the *ism* رُوَيْدَ (give grace/respite) resembles the word أَمْهِلْ, which is اَلْأَمْرُ الْحَاضِرُ الْمَعْرُوْفُ (one of the الْمَبْنِيُّ الْأَصْلُ) and has the same meaning.

   b. Resemblance in dependency. For example, the *ism* هٰذَا (اِسْمُ الْإِشَارَةِ), which is dependent on a مُشَارٌ إِلَيْهِ to give meaning, resembles a حَرْفٌ (one of the الْمَبْنِيُّ الْأَصْلُ), which is also dependent on another word to give meaning.

   c. Resemblance in having less than three letters. For example, the *ism* مَنْ, which is less than three letters, resembles حَرْفٌ (e.g. وَ), which is also generally less than three letters.

29

d. Resemblance in having had a حَرْفٌ originally. For example, the *ism* أَحَدَ عَشَرَ

resembles a حَرْفٌ in the sense that originally it contained a حَرْفٌ (أَحَدٌ وَعَشْرٌ).

*These three are known as اَلْمَبْنِيُّ الْأَصْلُ.

اَلْإِعْرَابُ الْمَحَلِّيّ:[15]

When a مَبْنِيّ word appears in a sentence in a place where it is supposed to be in the state of رَفْعٌ,

نَصْبٌ, جَرٌّ, or جَزْمٌ, its end does not change because it is مَبْنِيّ. However, it is said that it is in the

place of رَفْعٌ, نَصْبٌ, جَرٌّ, or جَزْمٌ (فِيْ مَحَلِّ رَفْعٍ أَوْ نَصْبٍ أَوْ جَرٍّ أَوْ جَزْمٍ), in accordance with its place in the

sentence.

For example,

نَصَرْنَاهُ   We helped him.

Keeping in mind that all pronouns are مَبْنِيّ, this sentence will be analyzed as follows:

نَصَرْ is فِعْلٌ مَاضٍ and is مَبْنِيٌّ عَلَى السُّكُوْنِ.

نَا is فَاعِلٌ, is مَبْنِيٌّ عَلَى السُّكُوْنِ and فِيْ مَحَلِّ رَفْعٍ.

ه is مَفْعُوْلٌ بِهِ, is مَبْنِيٌّ عَلَى الضَّمِّ and فِيْ مَحَلِّ نَصْبٍ.

EXERCISE

1. Analyze the following sentences like in the example given above.

i. قرأتُ هذا الكتاب

ii. ذهبتَ إلى عمه

iii. كتابه في بيته

---

[15] For more examples and exercises, please refer to *al-Nahw al-Wadih, Ibtida'iyyah*, vol. 2, 35-38.

Section 2.3

اَلْمُعْرَبُ – The declinable word

As mentioned above, a مُعْرَبٌ is a word whose end accepts any of the *i'raab* according to the requirement of the عَامِلٌ governing it.

e.g.	جَاءَ رَجُلٌ	رَأَيْتُ رَجُلًا	مَرَرْتُ بِرَجُلٍ
	A man came.	I saw a man.	I passed by a man.

Note: Here, the *i'raab* of رجل has changed according to the requirement of the عَامِلٌ.

<u>Types of مُعْرَبٌ:</u>

1. Amongst *fi'ls*, all of the *seeghahs* of فِعْلٌ مُضَارِعٌ besides those of جَمْعُ مُؤَنَّثٍ (حَاضِرٌ and غَائِبٌ) and those with نُونُ التَّأْكِيدِ (خَفِيفَةٌ and ثَقِيلَةٌ) are مُعْرَبٌ.

2. Amongst *isms*, those *isms* which accept *i'raab* changes are مُعْرَبٌ. They are known as مُتَمَكِّنٌ i.e. *isms* which give place to *i'raab* changes.

   <u>Note:</u> Such an *ism* is مُعْرَبٌ only when it is used in a sentence. If not used in a sentence, it is مَبْنِيٌّ. For example, بَيْت on its own, when not part of a sentence, is مَبْنِيٌّ عَلَى الضَّمِّ.

EXERCISES

1. State with reason whether the following words are مَبْنِيٌّ or مُعْرَبٌ.

i.	سَمِعَ	v.	يَكْسِرْنَ
ii.	مُنْذُ	vi.	لٰكِنَّ
iii.	يَنْصُرُ	vii.	ذٰلِكَ
iv.	يَضْرِبْنَ	viii.	اِسْمَعِي

2. Translate the following sentences and identify the مَبْنِيٌّ and مُعْرَبٌ words in them.

i.	نَظَرْتُ إِلَى الزَّهْرَةِ	v.	مَتَى يُسَافِرُ عَلِيٌّ؟
ii.	أَخَذْتُ الْكِتَابَ مِنَ الصَّدِيقِ	vi.	اَلْأَبُ فِي الدَّارِ
iii.	فَرِحَ الطَّالِبُ بِالنَّتِيجَةِ	vii.	اَلْوَلَدُ مُؤَدَّبٌ
iv.	كَيْفَ جَاءَ خَالِدٌ؟	viii.	اَللهُ يُحِبُّ الْمُحْسِنِينَ

31

Section 2.4

أَقْسَامُ الْأَسْمَاءِ الْمَبْنِيَّةِ – Types of indeclinable *isms*

The types of الْأَسْمَاءُ الْمَبْنِيَّةُ are as follows:

1. اَلضَّمَائِرُ (personal pronouns)

2. اَلْأَسْمَاءُ الْمَوْصُولَةُ (relative pronouns)

3. أَسْمَاءُ الْإِشَارَةِ (demonstrative pronouns)

4. أَسْمَاءُ الْأَفْعَالِ (*isms* that have the meaning of *fi'ls*)

5. أَسْمَاءُ الْأَصْوَاتِ (*isms* that denote a sound)

6. اَلظُّرُوفُ (adverbs)

7. اَلْكِنَايَاتُ (*isms* that indicate an unspecified quantity)

8. اَلْمُرَكَّبُ الْبِنَائِيُّ (numerical phrase)

In the following pages, we will look at each of these in detail.

<u>Section 2.4.1</u>[16]

<u>اَلضَّمَائِر – Personal pronouns</u>

We have discussed ضَمَائِر before. Now, we will look at them in greater detail.

<u>Definition</u>: A ضَمِيرٌ (plural: ضَمَائِر) is a word which is used in place of an اِسْمٌ and refers to the speaker (مُتَكَلِّمٌ) or the second person (حَاضِرٌ) or the third person (غَائِبٌ).

There are two types of ضَمَائِر:

1. اَلضَّمِيرُ الْبَارِز – Visible or independent pronoun: It is a ضَمِيرٌ which is visible and has a distinct form. It can appear on its own, i.e. unattached to another word, or it can be attached to another word. These two are defined as follows:

   i. اَلضَّمِيرُ الْمُنْفَصِل – Unattached pronoun: It is a ضَمِيرٌ which can be pronounced on its own without being connected to another word.

   ii. اَلضَّمِيرُ الْمُتَّصِل – Attached pronoun: It is a ضَمِيرٌ which cannot be pronounced on its own without being connected to another word.

2. اَلضَّمِيرُ الْمُسْتَتِر – Hidden or implied pronoun: It is a ضَمِيرٌ which is not visible but is implied. It is always مُتَّصِلٌ.

   <u>Note</u>: A hidden ضَمِيرٌ can only be in مَحَلِّ رَفْعٍ. (refer to اَلْإِعْرَابُ الْمَحَلِّيّ discussed above and Table 2.2 on the next page.)

Below are tables showing different forms that the ضَمَائِر will assume in the various conditions/states (*haalaat*).

---

[16] For more details, examples, and exercises, please refer to *al-Nahw al-Wadih*, *Ibtida'iyyah*, vol. 2, 120-135.

Table 2.1

ضَمِيرٌ مُنْفَصِلٌ بَارِزٌ فِي مَحَلِّ رَفْعٍ (ضَمِيرٌ مَرْفُوعٌ مُنْفَصِلٌ)

هُوَ	وَاحِدٌ مُذَكَّرٌ غَائِبٌ
هُمَا	تَثْنِيَةٌ مُذَكَّرٌ غَائِبٌ
هُمْ	جَمْعٌ مُذَكَّرٌ غَائِبٌ
هِيَ	وَاحِدٌ مُؤَنَّثٌ غَائِبٌ
هُمَا	تَثْنِيَةٌ مُؤَنَّثٌ غَائِبٌ
هُنَّ	جَمْعٌ مُؤَنَّثٌ غَائِبٌ
أَنْتَ	وَاحِدٌ مُذَكَّرٌ حَاضِرٌ
أَنْتُمَا	تَثْنِيَةٌ مُذَكَّرٌ حَاضِرٌ
أَنْتُمْ	جَمْعٌ مُذَكَّرٌ حَاضِرٌ
أَنْتِ	وَاحِدٌ مُؤَنَّثٌ حَاضِرٌ
أَنْتُمَا	تَثْنِيَةٌ مُؤَنَّثٌ حَاضِرٌ
أَنْتُنَّ	جَمْعٌ مُؤَنَّثٌ حَاضِرٌ
أَنَا	وَاحِدٌ مُتَكَلِّمٌ (مُذَكَّرٌ وَمُؤَنَّثٌ)
نَحْنُ	تَثْنِيَةٌ وَجَمْعٌ مُتَكَلِّمٌ (مُذَكَّرٌ وَمُؤَنَّثٌ)

e.g.

رَجُلٌ   هُوَ

خَبَرٌ   مُبْتَدَأٌ

(فِي مَحَلِّ رَفْعٍ)

Table 2.2

ضَمِيرٌ مُتَّصِلٌ فِي مَحَلِّ رَفْعٍ (ضَمِيرٌ مَرْفُوعٌ مُتَّصِلٌ)

بَارِزٌ		مُسْتَتِرٌ		
—	—	ضَرَبَ (هُوَ)	يَضْرِبُ (هُوَ)	وَاحِدٌ مُذَكَّرٌ غَائِبٌ
ضَرَبَا (ا)	يَضْرِبَانِ (ا)	—	—	تَثْنِيَةٌ مُذَكَّرٌ غَائِبٌ
ضَرَبُوا (و)	يَضْرِبُونَ (و)	—	—	جَمْعٌ مُذَكَّرٌ غَائِبٌ
—	—	ضَرَبَتْ (هِيَ)	تَضْرِبُ (هِيَ)	وَاحِدٌ مُؤَنَّثٌ غَائِبٌ
ضَرَبَتَا (ا)	تَضْرِبَانِ (ا)	—	—	تَثْنِيَةٌ مُؤَنَّثٌ غَائِبٌ
ضَرَبْنَ (ن)	يَضْرِبْنَ (ن)	—	—	جَمْعٌ مُؤَنَّثٌ غَائِبٌ
ضَرَبْتَ (تَ)	—	—	تَضْرِبُ (أَنْتَ)	وَاحِدٌ مُذَكَّرٌ حَاضِرٌ
ضَرَبْتُمَا (تُمَا)	تَضْرِبَانِ (ا)	—	—	تَثْنِيَةٌ مُذَكَّرٌ حَاضِرٌ
ضَرَبْتُمْ (تُمْ)	تَضْرِبُونَ (و)	—	—	جَمْعٌ مُذَكَّرٌ حَاضِرٌ
ضَرَبْتِ (ت)	تَضْرِبِينَ (ي)	—	—	وَاحِدٌ مُؤَنَّثٌ حَاضِرٌ
ضَرَبْتُمَا (تُمَا)	تَضْرِبَانِ (ا)	—	—	تَثْنِيَةٌ مُؤَنَّثٌ حَاضِرٌ
ضَرَبْتُنَّ (تُنَّ)	تَضْرِبْنَ (ن)	—	—	جَمْعٌ مُؤَنَّثٌ حَاضِرٌ
ضَرَبْتُ (تُ)	—	—	أَضْرِبُ (أَنَا)	وَاحِدٌ مُتَكَلِّمٌ (مُذَكَّرٌ وَمُؤَنَّثٌ)
ضَرَبْنَا (نَا)	—	—	نَضْرِبُ (نَحْنُ)	تَثْنِيَةٌ وَجَمْعٌ مُتَكَلِّمٌ (مُذَكَّرٌ وَمُؤَنَّثٌ)

Note: In the table above, the ضَمِيرٌ مُتَّصِلٌ which in many cases is the فَاعِلٌ is indicated after its respective *fiʿl* in parentheses.

Table 2.3

ضَمِيرٌ مُتَّصِلٌ وَضَمِيرٌ مُنْفَصِلٌ فِي مَحَلِّ نَصْبٍ (ضَمِيرٌ مَنْصُوبٌ مُتَّصِلٌ وَضَمِيرٌ مَنْصُوبٌ مُنْفَصِلٌ)

	ضَمِيرٌ مَنْصُوبٌ مُتَّصِلٌ بَارِزٌ		ضَمِيرٌ مَنْصُوبٌ مُنْفَصِلٌ بَارِزٌ
	Example	*Dameer*	
وَاحِدٌ مُذَكَّرٌ غَائِبٌ	ضَرَبَهُ	ه	إِيَّاهُ
تَثْنِيَةٌ مُذَكَّرٌ غَائِبٌ	ضَرَبَهُمَا	هما	إِيَّاهُمَا
جَمْعٌ مُذَكَّرٌ غَائِبٌ	ضَرَبَهُمْ	هم	إِيَّاهُمْ
وَاحِدٌ مُؤَنَّثٌ غَائِبٌ	ضَرَبَهَا	ها	إِيَّاهَا
تَثْنِيَةٌ مُؤَنَّثٌ غَائِبٌ	ضَرَبَهُمَا	هما	إِيَّاهُمَا
جَمْعٌ مُؤَنَّثٌ غَائِبٌ	ضَرَبَهُنَّ	هن	إِيَّاهُنَّ
وَاحِدٌ مُذَكَّرٌ حَاضِرٌ	ضَرَبَكَ	ك	إِيَّاكَ
تَثْنِيَةٌ مُذَكَّرٌ حَاضِرٌ	ضَرَبَكُمَا	كما	إِيَّاكُمَا
جَمْعٌ مُذَكَّرٌ حَاضِرٌ	ضَرَبَكُمْ	كم	إِيَّاكُمْ
وَاحِدٌ مُؤَنَّثٌ حَاضِرٌ	ضَرَبَكِ	ك	إِيَّاكِ
تَثْنِيَةٌ مُؤَنَّثٌ حَاضِرٌ	ضَرَبَكُمَا	كما	إِيَّاكُمَا
جَمْعٌ مُؤَنَّثٌ حَاضِرٌ	ضَرَبَكُنَّ	كن	إِيَّاكُنَّ
وَاحِدٌ مُتَكَلِّمٌ (مُذَكَّرٌ وَمُؤَنَّثٌ)	ضَرَبَنِي [17]	ي	إِيَّايَ
تَثْنِيَةٌ وَجَمْعٌ مُتَكَلِّمٌ (مُذَكَّرٌ وَمُؤَنَّثٌ)	ضَرَبَنَا	نا	إِيَّانَا

e.g.   <u>نَعْبُدُ</u>   <u>إِيَّاكَ</u>   You alone we worship.

فِعْلٌ مَعَ فَاعِلِهِ   مَفْعُولٌ مُقَدَّمٌ (فِي مَحَلِّ نَصْبٍ)

---

[17] Sometimes, a ن (نُونُ الْوِقَايَةِ) is added before the ضَمِيرٌ يَاء to protect an *i'raab* as in ضَرَبَنِي, which would otherwise be incorrectly read as ضَرَبِي (the لَام كَلِمَة of ٱلْفِعْلُ ٱلْمَاضِيْ is مَبْنِيٌّ عَلَى الْفَتْحِ).

36

There are two ways in which ضَمِيرٌ مُتَّصِلٌ بَارِزٌ appears in مَحَلِّ جَرٍّ. One is when it is preceded by a حَرْفُ جَرٍّ, and the other is when some other word is مُضَافٌ to it.

Table 2.4

ضَمِيرٌ مُتَّصِلٌ بَارِزٌ فِي مَحَلِّ جَرٍّ (ضَمِيرٌ مَجْرُورٌ مُتَّصِلٌ)

بِحَرْفِ الْجَرِّ	بِالْإِضَافَةِ	
لَهُ	دَارُهُ	وَاحِدٌ مُذَكَّرٌ غَائِبٌ
لَهُمَا	دَارُهُمَا	تَثْنِيَةٌ مُذَكَّرٌ غَائِبٌ
لَهُمْ	دَارُهُمْ	جَمْعٌ مُذَكَّرٌ غَائِبٌ
لَهَا	دَارُهَا	وَاحِدٌ مُؤَنَّثٌ غَائِبٌ
لَهُمَا	دَارُهُمَا	تَثْنِيَةٌ مُؤَنَّثٌ غَائِبٌ
لَهُنَّ	دَارُهُنَّ	جَمْعٌ مُؤَنَّثٌ غَائِبٌ
لَكَ	دَارُكَ	وَاحِدٌ مُذَكَّرٌ حَاضِرٌ
لَكُمَا	دَارُكُمَا	تَثْنِيَةٌ مُذَكَّرٌ حَاضِرٌ
لَكُمْ	دَارُكُمْ	جَمْعٌ مُذَكَّرٌ حَاضِرٌ
لَكِ	دَارُكِ	وَاحِدٌ مُؤَنَّثٌ حَاضِرٌ
لَكُمَا	دَارُكُمَا	تَثْنِيَةٌ مُؤَنَّثٌ حَاضِرٌ
لَكُنَّ	دَارُكُنَّ	جَمْعٌ مُؤَنَّثٌ حَاضِرٌ
لِي	دَارِي	وَاحِدٌ مُتَكَلِّمٌ (مُذَكَّرٌ وَمُؤَنَّثٌ)
لَنَا	دَارُنَا	تَثْنِيَةٌ وَجَمْعٌ مُتَكَلِّمٌ (مُذَكَّرٌ وَمُؤَنَّثٌ)

e.g.   لَهُ   دَارُهُ   His house is his.

حَرْفُ جَرٍّ + مَجْرُورٌ   مُضَافٌ + مُضَافٌ إِلَيْهِ

(ضَمِيرٌ مُتَّصِلٌ مَجْرُورٌ بِحَرْفِ الْجَرِّ)   (ضَمِيرٌ مُتَّصِلٌ مَجْرُورٌ بِالْإِضَافَةِ)

Note: The ضَمِيرٌ بَارِزٌ in مَحَلِّ جَرٍّ will always be مُتَّصِلٌ.

37

<u>ضَمِيرُ الشَّأْن</u>:

It is a singular ضَمِيرٌ غَائِبٌ مُذَكَّرٌ which sometimes appears at the beginning of a sentence without a مَرْجَعٌ (an earlier word that it could refer to). The sentence after it clarifies such a ضَمِيرٌ.

إِنَّهُ زَيْدٌ قَائِمٌ   e.g.   Indeed, the matter is that Zayd is standing.

<u>ضَمِيرُ الْقِصَّة</u>:

It is a singular ضَمِيرٌ غَائِبٌ مُؤَنَّثٌ which sometimes appears at the beginning of a sentence without a مَرْجَعٌ (an earlier word that it could refer to). The sentence after it clarifies such a ضَمِيرٌ.

إِنَّهَا فَاطِمَةُ قَائِمَةٌ   e.g.   Indeed, the matter is that Fatimah is standing.

<u>ضَمِيرُ الْفَصْل</u>:

It is a ضَمِيرٌ which appears between a مُبْتَدَأٌ and a خَبَرٌ for emphasis and separation.

أُولَٰئِكَ هُمُ الْمُفْلِحُونَ   e.g.   It is they who are successful.

EXERCISE

1. Translate, fill in the *i'raab* and analyze the following sentences, pointing out all the ضَمَائِر, as well as their types and حَالَاتٌ.

iii. اَلشُّرْطِيُّ نَصَرَنَا   i. القطار قدم في وقته

iv. الله يرزقها وإياكم   ii. نحن نرزقك

<u>Section 2.4.2</u>[18]

<u>اَلْأَسْمَاءُ الْمَوْصُوْلَةُ</u> - Relative pronouns

<u>Definition:</u> An اِسْمٌ مَوْصُوْلٌ is an اِسْمٌ مَعْرِفَةٌ whose meaning/purpose is understood through the sentence, which comes after it, which is called صِلَةٌ.

■ An اِسْمٌ مَوْصُوْلٌ cannot form a complete part of a sentence on its own. It must have a صِلَةٌ which relates (refers back) to it. The صِلَةٌ which is generally a جُمْلَةٌ خَبَرِيَّةٌ must have a ضَمِيْرٌ (visible or hidden) referring to the اِسْمٌ مَوْصُوْلٌ. This ضَمِيْرٌ is called عَائِدٌ.

Table 2.5

اَلْأَسْمَاءُ الْمَوْصُوْلَةُ لِلْمُذَكَّرِ

وَاحِدٌ	اَلَّذِيْ	who, that, which	
تَثْنِيَةٌ	اَللَّذَانِ	those two who, that, which	فِيْ مَحَلِّ رَفْعٍ
تَثْنِيَةٌ	اَللَّذَيْنِ	those two who, that, which	فِيْ مَحَلِّ نَصْبٍ وَجَرٍّ
جَمْعٌ	اَلَّذِيْنَ	those who, that, which	

Table 2.6

اَلْأَسْمَاءُ الْمَوْصُوْلَةُ لِلْمُؤَنَّثِ

وَاحِدٌ	اَلَّتِيْ	who, that, which	
تَثْنِيَةٌ	اَللَّتَانِ	those two who, that, which	فِيْ مَحَلِّ رَفْعٍ
تَثْنِيَةٌ	اَللَّتَيْنِ	those two who, that, which	فِيْ مَحَلِّ نَصْبٍ وَجَرٍّ
جَمْعٌ	اَللَّائِيْ	those who, that, which	
جَمْعٌ	اَللَّوَاتِيْ	those who, that, which	

Examples

1. جَاءَ الَّذِيْ نَصَرَكَ — **The one** (masculine) who helped you, came.

2. جَاءَ الَّذَانِ نَصَرَاكَ — **The two** (masculine) who helped you, came.

3. رَأَيْتُ اللَّذَيْنِ نَصَرَاكَ — I saw **the two** (masculine) who helped you.

4. لَقِيْتُ الَّذِيْنَ نَصَرُوْنِيْ — I met **those** (masculine) who helped me.

5. جَاءَتِ الَّتِيْ نَصَرَتْكَ — **The one** (feminine) who helped you, came.

6. جَاءَتِ اللَّتَانِ نَصَرَتَاكَ — **The two** (feminine) who helped you, came.

---

[18] For more examples and exercises, please refer to *al-Nahw al-Wadih*, *Ibtida'iyyah*, vol. 2, 136-140.

7. رَأَيْتُ **اللَّتَيْنِ** نَصَرَتَاكَ	I saw **the two** (feminine) who helped you.	
8. جَاءَتِ **اللَّائِيْ** نَصَرْنَكَ	**Those** (feminine) who helped you, came.	

Additional relative pronouns:

1. مَا and مَنْ (that and who)
   - These are used for all genders and all numbers.
   - The difference is that مَنْ is used for intelligent beings (ذَوِى الْعُقُوْلِ) and مَا is used for non-intelligent beings (غَيْرُ ذَوِى الْعُقُوْلِ).

e.g.	أَحْسِنْ اِلٰى مَنْ أَحْسَنَ إِلَيْكَ	Show goodness to that person who has shown goodness to you.
	قَرَأْتُ مَا كَتَبْتَ	I read what you wrote.

2. أَيٌّ and أَيَّةٌ
   - They are generally مُعْرَبٌ and used in إِضَافَةٌ.
   - أَيٌّ has the meaning of اَلَّذِيْ.

e.g.	مِنْ أَيِّ كِتَابٍ	from which book…

   - أَيَّةٌ has the meaning of اَلَّتِيْ.

e.g.	أَيَّةُ بِنْتٍ	which girl…

3. ال which appears before an اِسْمُ فَاعِلٍ and an اِسْمُ مَفْعُوْلٍ, has the effect of اِسْمٌ مَوْصُوْلٌ.

e.g.	اَلسَّامِعُ	would equal	اَلَّذِيْ سَمِعَ
	اَلْمَسْمُوْعُ	would equal	اَلَّذِيْ سُمِعَ
	اَلسَّامِعُوْنَ	would equal	اَلَّذِيْنَ سَمِعُوْا

4. ذُوْ

According to the dialect of the tribe بَنُوْ طَيِّ, it is an اِسْمٌ مَوْصُوْلٌ.
It is used for all genders and all numbers, without its form changing.

e.g.	جَاءَ ذُوْ نَصَرَكَ	equals	جَاءَ الَّذِيْ نَصَرَكَ	The one who helped you, came.
	رَأَيْتُ ذُوْ نَصَرَكَ	equals	رَأَيْتُ الَّذِيْ نَصَرَكَ	I saw the one who helped you.
	مَرَرْتُ بِذُوْ نَصَرَكَ	equals	مَرَرْتُ بِالَّذِيْ نَصَرَكَ	I passed by the one who helped you.

40

Sentence Analysis:

جَاءَ الَّذِيْ أَبُوْهُ عَالِمٌ The person whose father is knowledgeable, came.

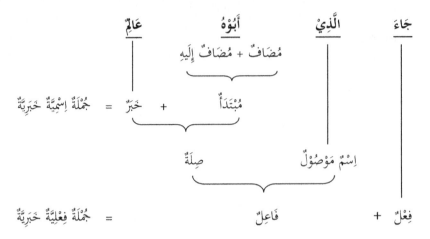

EXERCISE

1. Translate, fill in the *i'raab*, and analyze the following sentences.

   i. ‏أين الذي نصر زيدا؟‏

   ii. ‏الله يعلم ما في الأرض‏

   iii. ‏جاءت اللتان تسكنان أمامنا‏

   iv. ‏إن الذين كفروا لا يدخلون الجنة‏

41

أَسْمَاءُ الْإِشَارَة – Demonstrative *isms*

Definition: An إِسْمُ الْإِشَارَة is an إِسْمٌ which is used to point at something. This إِسْمٌ is of two types.

i. لِلْقَرِيبِ: It is used for pointing at something near.

ii. لِلْبَعِيدِ: It is used for pointing at something far.

Table 2.7

أَسْمَاءُ الْإِشَارَة لِلْمُذَكَّرِ

	لِلْقَرِيبِ			لِلْبَعِيدِ		
وَاحِدٌ	هٰذَا	this		ذٰلِكَ	that	
تَثْنِيَةٌ	هٰذَانِ	these two…	حَالَةُ الرَّفْع	ذَانِكَ	those two…	حَالَةُ الرَّفْع
تَثْنِيَةٌ	هٰذَيْنِ	these two…	حَالَةُ النَّصْبِ وَالْجَرِّ	ذَيْنِكَ	those two…	حَالَةُ النَّصْبِ وَالْجَرِّ
جَمْعٌ	هٰؤُلَاءِ	these		أُولٰئِكَ	those	

Table 2.8

أَسْمَاءُ الْإِشَارَة لِلْمُؤَنَّث

	لِلْقَرِيبِ			لِلْبَعِيدِ		
وَاحِدٌ	هٰذِهِ	this		تِلْكَ	that	
تَثْنِيَةٌ	هَاتَانِ	these two…	حَالَةُ الرَّفْع	تَانِكَ	those two…	حَالَةُ الرَّفْع
تَثْنِيَةٌ	هَاتَيْنِ	these two…	حَالَةُ النَّصْبِ وَالْجَرِّ	تَيْنِكَ	those two…	حَالَةُ النَّصْبِ وَالْجَرِّ
جَمْعٌ	هٰؤُلَاءِ	these		أُولٰئِكَ	those	

e.g.

ذٰلِكَ الْكِتَابُ	that book
هٰؤُلَاءِ النِّسَاءُ	these women
أُولٰئِكَ الرِّجَالُ	those men

---

[19] For more examples and exercises, please refer to *al-Nahw al-Wadih, Ibtida'iyyah*, vol. 2, 141-145.

Notes:

1. In the case of أَسْمَاءُ الْإِشَارَةِ لِلْقَرِيْبِ, for both masculine and feminine, the هـ in the beginning is not part of the actual اِسْمُ الْإِشَارَةِ. It is, in fact, a حَرْفُ تَنْبِيْهٍ. However, it is so often used with the أَسْمَاءُ الْإِشَارَةِ لِلْقَرِيْبِ that it is normally considered a part of them.

2. The كَ of اِسْمُ الْإِشَارَةِ (اَلْبَعِيْدُ) is sometimes changed according to the gender or the number of persons being addressed. The meaning is not affected.

   e.g.   ذٰلِكُمَا رَبُّكُمَا   He is the Lord of both of you.

3. If the مُشَارٌ إِلَيْهِ is a مُضَافٌ, then the اِسْمُ الْإِشَارَةِ comes after the مُضَافٌ إِلَيْهِ.

   e.g.   كِتَابُكَ هٰذَا   this book of yours

4. If the اِسْمُ الْإِشَارَةِ occurs as a مُبْتَدَأٌ, then the خَبَرٌ is generally a نَكِرَةٌ.

   e.g.   هٰذَا كِتَابٌ   This is a book.

   However, if the خَبَرٌ is also مَعْرِفَةٌ, then a suitable ضَمِيْرٌ should be added between the مُبْتَدَأٌ, which is an اِسْمُ الْإِشَارَةِ, and the خَبَرٌ for it to remain a complete sentence.

   e.g.   هٰذَا هُوَ الْكِتَابُ   This is the book.

   If no ضَمِيْرٌ is added, it would be an incomplete sentence.

   e.g.   هٰذَا الْكِتَابُ   this book

5. If the خَبَرٌ is a مُضَافٌ, then there will be no need for a ضَمِيْرٌ to be added between the مُبْتَدَأٌ and the خَبَرٌ.

   e.g.   هٰذَا ابْنُ الْمَلِكِ   This is the son of the king.

6. هُنَا or هٰهُنَا (here) and هُنَاكَ (there) are also أَسْمَاءُ الْإِشَارَةِ. However, they do not have any special rules.

Sentence Analysis:

نَفِيْسٌ   الْقَلَمُ   هٰذَا   This pen is precious.

اِسْمُ الْإِشَارَةِ   +   مُشَارٌ إِلَيْهِ

خَبَرٌ   +   مُبْتَدَأٌ   =   جُمْلَةٌ اِسْمِيَّةٌ خَبَرِيَّةٌ

EXERCISE

1. Translate, fill in the *i'raab*, and analyze the following sentences.

i.	تلك السيارة قديمة	iv.	هذه حجرة واسعة
ii.	أولئك تجار صادقون	v.	هذان ولدان مهذبان
iii.	هؤلاء طلاب المدرسة	vi.	هذان الولدان مهذبان

Section 2.4.4[20]

أَسْمَاءُ الْأَفْعَال —*Isms* that have the meaning of *fi'ls*

<u>Definition:</u> These are *isms* that have the meaning of *fi'ls* but do not accept their signs.

- Some of them have the meaning of الْفِعْلُ الْمَاضِي and give the إِسْمٌ after it a *raf'*; and the one which has the meaning of الْأَمْرُ الْحَاضِرُ, gives the إِسْمٌ after it a *nasb*.

Table 2.9
Isms in the Meaning of الْفِعْلُ الْمَاضِي

Ism	*Fi'l*	Meaning	Example	
هَيْهَاتَ	بَعُدَ	he/it became far, it is far (from him)	هَيْهَاتَ زَيْدٌ أَنْ يَفْعَلَ هٰذَا	It is far from (beyond) Zayd to do this.
شَتَّانَ	بَعُدَ وَ افْتَرَقَ	same as above; and what a difference, there is a difference between	شَتَّانَ بَيْنَ الْعَالِمِ وَالْجَاهِلِ	What a difference there is between the learned and the ignorant!
سَرْعَانَ	سَرُعَ	he hastened	سَرْعَانَ زَيْدٌ	Zayd hastened.

Table 2.10
Isms in the Meaning of الْأَمْرُ الْحَاضِرُ

Ism	*Fi'l*	Meaning	Example	
رُوَيْدَ	أَمْهِلْ	Give respite!	رُوَيْدَ زَيْدًا	Give Zayd respite.
بَلْهَ	دَعْ	Leave!; Give up!	بَلْهَ التَّفَكُّرَ فِيْمَا لَا يَعْنِيْكَ	Give up thinking about that which does not concern you.
دُوْنَكَ – هَا	خُذْ	Take!	دُوْنَكَ اللَّبَنَ	Take the milk.
عَلَيْكَ	الْزَمْ	Hold on to (it)!; (It is) incumbent on you	عَلَيْكَ بِسُنَّتِي	Hold on to my Sunnah.
حَيَّهَلْ – حَيَّ هَيْتَ – هَلُمَّ	إِئْتِ – عَجِّلْ أَقْبِلْ	Come!; Hasten!	حَيَّ عَلَى الصَّلَاةِ	Come to *salah*.

---

[20] For more examples and exercises, please refer to 'Ali al-Jaarim & Mustafa Ameen, *al-Nahw al-Wadih li al-Madaris al-Thanawiyyah*, (Cairo: Dar al-Ma'arif, n.d.), vol. 1, 40-43.

Notes:

1. There are some other *isms* which have the meaning of *fiʿls*. These are as follows:

   تَعَالَ   (اِئْتِ – come)   أمِيْنَ (اِسْتَجِبْ – accept)

   صَهْ   (اُسْكُتْ – keep quite)   فَقَطْ (اِكْتَفِ – suffice)

   هَاتِ   (اِعْطِ – bring, give)   إلَيْكَ عَنِّيْ (تَبَعَّدْ عَنِّيْ – away from me)

   عَلَيَّ بِهِ   (جِئْ بِهِ عِنْدِيْ – bring him/it to me)

2. Some of these *isms* are inflectable (مُتَصَرِّفٌ), i.e. their form changes.

   i.   هَاتِ   هَاتِيَا   هَاتُوْا   هَاتِيْ   هَاتِيَا   هَاتِيْنَ

   e.g.   قُلْ هَاتُوْا بُرْهَنَكُمْ إنْ كُنْتُمْ صٰدِقِيْنَ

   Say: bring your proof, if you are truthful.

   ii.   تَعَالَ   تَعَالَيَا   تَعَالَوْا   تَعَالَيْ   تَعَالَيَا   تَعَالَيْنَ

   e.g.   قُلْ يٰأَهْلَ الْكِتٰبِ تَعَالَوْا إلٰى كَلِمَةٍ...الآية[21]

   Say: O people of the book! Come to a word…

   e.g.   فَتَعَالَيْنَ أُمَتِّعْكُنَّ وَأُسَرِّحْكُنَّ سَرَاحًا جَمِيْلًا (القرآن)

   Then, come, I will make provision for you and release you with kindness.

Section 2.4.5
أَسْمَاءُ الْأَصْوَات – *Isms* that denote a sound

أُحْ أُحْ	To denote a cough.
أُفْ	To denote pain.
بَخْ	To denote happiness, pleasure.
نَخَّ	To make a camel sit.
غَاقَ	To denote the cawing of a crow.

---

[21] الآية is an abbreviation for إلٰى آخِرِ الْآيَةِ (until the end of the *ayah*).

Section 2.4.6[22]
اَلظُّرُوفُ – Adverbs

<u>Definition:</u> An اِسْمُ ظَرْفٍ is an اِسْمٌ which gives us an idea of the place or time when (or where) some work is done. It is also called مَفْعُولٌ فِيهِ.

ظُرُوفٌ are of two kinds: ظَرْفُ الزَّمَانِ (adverb of time) and ظَرْفُ الْمَكَانِ (the adverb of place).

ظُرُوفُ الزَّمَانِ – Adverbs of time:

1. إِذْ   (when)

   - It gives the meaning of اَلْمَاضِي even when it appears before فِعْلٌ مُضَارِعٌ.
   - The sentence after إِذْ could be a جُمْلَةٌ اِسْمِيَّةٌ or a جُمْلَةٌ فِعْلِيَّةٌ.

     e.g.   وَاذْكُرُوا إِذْ أَنْتُمْ قَلِيلٌ   Remember when you were less.

     e.g.   وَإِذْ يَرْفَعُ إِبْرَاهِيمُ الْقَوَاعِدَ مِنَ الْبَيْتِ   And when Ibrahim (Allah give him peace) was raising the foundation of the House (Ka'ba).

   - Sometimes, it gives the meaning of suddenness (مُفَاجَأَةٌ). This is called إِذِ الْفُجَائِيَّةُ.

     e.g.   خَرَجْتُ إِذْ مُدِيرُ الْمَدْرَسَةِ نَاظِرٌ   I came out and suddenly (encountered) the principal of the school watching.

   - Sometimes, it gives the meaning of because (لِأَنَّ). This is called إِذِ التَّعْلِيلِيَّةُ.

     e.g.   لَنْ يَّنْفَعَكُمُ الْيَوْمَ إِذْ ظَلَمْتُمْ أَنَّكُمْ فِي الْعَذَابِ مُشْتَرِكُونَ (القرآن)

     That you are together in punishment will never benefit you today because you oppressed.

     [This is according to one translation.]

2. إِذَا   (when/if)

   - It gives the meaning of مُضَارِعٌ even when it appears before فِعْلٌ مَاضٍ.
   - It gives the meaning of شَرْطٌ and جَزَاءٌ but does not give either a جَزْمٌ.
   - The sentence after إِذَا could be a جُمْلَةٌ اِسْمِيَّةٌ or preferably a جُمْلَةٌ فِعْلِيَّةٌ.

     e.g.   آتِيكَ إِذَا الشَّمْسُ طَالِعَةٌ   I will come to you when the sun is up.

     e.g.   إِذَا نَزَلَ الْمَطَرُ فَارْجِعْ إِلَى الْبَيْتِ   If it rains, return home.

---

[22] The list of ظُرُوفٌ given in this section is by no means exhaustive. There are many more that should be studied in advanced books of *Nahw*.

e.g.   إِذَا جَاءَ نَصْرُ اللهِ وَالْفَتْحُ وَرَأَيْتَ النَّاسَ يَدْخُلُونَ فِيْ دِيْنِ اللهِ أَفْوَاجاً فَسَبِّحْ بِحَمْدِ رَبِّكَ وَاسْتَغْفِرْهُ

When the victory of Allah comes and the conquest, and you see people entering into the religion of Allah in multitudes, then celebrate the praise of your Lord and seek forgiveness from Him.

- Sometimes, it gives the meaning of suddenness (مُفَاجَأَةٌ), in which case إِذَا must be followed by a جُمْلَةٌ اِسْمِيَّةٌ.

  e.g.   خَرَجْتُ فَإِذَا الْكَلْبُ وَاقِفٌ   I came out and suddenly (encountered) the dog standing.

3. مَتَى (when)

   - It can be used as an interrogative (اِسْتِفْهَامٌ).

     e.g.   مَتَى تُسَافِرُ؟   When will you travel?

   - It can also be used as a conditional اِسْمٌ in which case the شَرْطٌ and جَزَاءٌ get a جَزْمٌ.

     e.g.   مَتَى تَصُمْ أَصُمْ   When you fast, I will fast.

4. كَيْفَ (how)

   - It is used to enquire condition.

     e.g.   كَيْفَ حَالُكَ؟   How are you? (In what condition are you?)

5. أَيَّانَ (when)

   - It is used as an interrogative.

     e.g.   أَيَّانَ يَوْمُ الدِّيْنِ؟   When will be the day of recompense?

   Note: أَيَّانَ is used only to enquire of great events of the future as compared to مَتَى.

6. أَمْسِ (yesterday)

   e.g.   جَاءَنِيْ زَيْدٌ أَمْسِ   Zayd came to me yesterday.

7. مُنْذُ – مُذْ (since, for)

   - These two can be used to convey the beginning of a time period.

     e.g.   مَا رَأَيْتُهُ مُنْذُ/مُذْ يَوْمِ الْجُمُعَةِ   I have not seen him since Friday.

   - They can also be used to refer to an entire time period.

     e.g.   مَا رَأَيْتُهُ مُنْذُ/مُذْ يَوْمَيْنِ   I have not seen him for two days.

- These can be used as حَرْفُ جَرٍّ (followed by a مَجْرُورٌ) **or** as اِسْمٌ which is regarded as a مُبْتَدَأً followed by a مَرْفُوعٌ.

  e.g.   مَا رَأَيْتُهُ مُنْذُ/مُذْ يَوْمِ الْجُمُعَةِ   I have not seen him since Friday.

      مَا رَأَيْتُهُ مُنْذُ/مُذْ يَوْمُ الْجُمُعَةِ

8. قَطُّ   (not, never)

  - It is used to emphasize الْمَاضِيْ الْمَنْفِيُّ.

    e.g.   مَا ضَرَبْتُهُ قَطُّ   I never hit him.

9. عَوْضُ   (never)

  - It is used to emphasize الْمُضَارِعُ الْمَنْفِيُّ.

    e.g.   لَا أَضْرِبُهُ عَوْضُ   I will never hit him.

10. قَبْلُ   (before)

  بَعْدُ   (after)

  - They are مُعْرَبٌ when they are مُضَافٌ and the مُضَافٌ إِلَيْهِ is mentioned.

    e.g.   مِنْ قَبْلِ الْفَتْحِ   before the victory

  - They are مَبْنِيٌّ when they are مُضَافٌ and the مُضَافٌ إِلَيْهِ is not mentioned, but intended.

    e.g.   لِلَّهِ الْأَمْرُ مِنْ قَبْلُ وَمِنْ بَعْدُ (أَيْ مِنْ قَبْلِ كُلِّ شَيْءٍ وَمِنْ بَعْدِ كُلِّ شَيْءٍ)

    Allah's is the decision before and after (i.e. before everything and after everything).

    e.g.   أَنَا حَاضِرٌ مِنْ قَبْلُ (أَيْ مِنْ قَبْلِكَ)

    I have been present from before (i.e. before you).

    e.g.   مَتَى تَجِيئُنَا بَعْدُ؟ (أَيْ بَعْدَ هٰذَا)

    When will you come after (i.e. after this)?

ظُرُوفُ الْمَكَانِ – Adverbs of place:

1. حَيْثُ   (where)

  - It is generally مُضَافٌ to a sentence.

    e.g.   اِجْلِسْ حَيْثُ زَيْدٌ جَالِسٌ   Sit where Zayd is sitting.

2. قُدَّامُ (in front of) & خَلْفُ (behind)

- It has the same rules as those for قَبْلُ and بَعْدُ.

  e.g. قَامَ النَّاسُ قُدَّامُ وَخَلْفُ (أَيْ قُدَّامَهُ وَخَلْفَهُ)

  The people stood in front and behind.
  (i.e. in front of him and behind him).

3. تَحْتُ (under) & فَوْقُ (on top, above)

- It has the same rules as those for قَبْلُ and بَعْدُ.

  e.g. جَلَسَ زَيْدٌ تَحْتُ وَعَمْرٌو فَوْقُ (أَيْ تَحْتَ الشَّجَرَةِ وَفَوْقَ الشَّجَرَةِ)

  Zayd sat under and 'Amr above. (i.e. under the tree and above the tree.)

4. عِنْدَ (by, at, near, with)

  e.g. اَلْمَالُ عِنْدَ زَيْدٍ   The money is with Zayd.

  Note: عِنْدَ will get a *kasrah* if it is preceded by مِنْ.

  e.g. مِنْ عِنْدِ اللهِ   from Allah

5. أَيْنَ/أَنَّى (where)

- They are used for اِسْتِفْهَامٌ.

  e.g. أَنَّى تَذْهَبُ – أَيْنَ تَذْهَبُ؟ Where are you going?

- They are used for شَرْطٌ (شَرْطٌ and جَزَاءٌ will get a جَزْمٌ).

  e.g. أَيْنَ تَجْلِسْ أَجْلِسْ   Where you sit, I will sit.

  أَنَّى تَجْلِسْ أَجْلِسْ

6. لَدَى/لَدُنْ (at, by, near, with (same meaning as عِنْدَ)).

  e.g. اَلْمَالُ لَدَى زَيْدٍ   The money is with Zayd.

  مِنْ لَدُنْ حَكِيمٍ خَبِيرٍ   from the All-Wise, All-Knowing

- لَدُنْ is generally preceded by مِنْ.

- When used in the meaning of possession (with), the difference between لَدَى/لَدُنْ and عِنْدَ is that in the case of لَدُنْ/لَدَى, the possessed thing must be present with the person; whereas, in the case of عِنْدَ, the possessed thing need not be present with the person.

50

Note: That adverb which is مُعْرَبٌ and is مُضَافٌ to a sentence or the word إِذْ, could be مَبْنِيٌّ عَلَى الْفَتْحِ **or** it could get the *i'raab* according to the عَامِلٌ.

e.g. the adverb يوم which is مُضَافٌ in the following *ayahs*:

هٰذَا يَوْمُ يَنْفَعُ الصَّادِقِينَ صِدْقُهُمْ and هٰذَا يَوْمَ يَنْفَعُ الصَّادِقِينَ صِدْقُهُمْ

This is the day when the truth of the truthful will benefit them.

وُجُوهٌ يَّوْمَئِذٍ and وُجُوهٌ يَّوْمَئِذٍ

faces on that day

EXERCISE

1. Translate the follows *ayahs* of the Qur'an and identify the ظُرُوفٌ in them. Also identify whether they are from among ظُرُوفُ الْمَكَانِ or ظُرُوفُ الزَّمَانِ.

i. يَوْمَ يَكُونُ النَّاسُ كَالْفَرَاشِ الْمَبْثُوثِ

ii. وَمَا جَعَلْنَا لِبَشَرٍ مِّنْ قَبْلِكَ الْخُلْدَ

iii. فَسُبْحَانَ اللهِ حِينَ تُمْسُونَ وَحِينَ تُصْبِحُونَ

iv. قَالَ فَإِنَّا قَدْ فَتَنَّا قَوْمَكَ مِنْ بَعْدِكَ

v. إِذْ جَاؤُوكُمْ مِنْ فَوْقِكُمْ

vi. مَا عِنْدِي مَا تَسْتَعْجِلُونَ بِهِ

vii. وَعَلَّمْنَاهُ مِنْ لَّدُنَّا عِلْماً

viii. يَعْلَمُ مَا بَيْنَ أَيْدِيهِمْ وَمَا خَلْفَهُمْ

ix. إِذْ يَقُولُ لِصَاحِبِهِ لَا تَحْزَنْ إِنَّ اللهَ مَعَنَا

x. أَعَدَّ اللهُ لَهُمْ جَنَّاتٍ تَجْرِي مِنْ تَحْتِهَا الْأَنْهَارُ

Section 2.4.7

<u>اَلْكِنَايَاتُ</u> – *Isms* that indicate an unspecified quantity

1. كَمْ، كَذَا   (so many, so much, how many, how much)

   - They can be used for numbers

     e.g.   كَمْ دِرْهَمًا عِنْدَكَ؟ How many silver coins do you have?

     e.g.   أَخَذْتُ كَذَا دِرْهَمًا   I took this many silver coins.

   - كَذَا is also used in the meaning of "such and such."

     e.g.   قَالَ لِي كَذَا وَ كَذَا   He said to me such and such.

2. كَيْتَ، ذَيْتَ   (so and so, such and such)

   e.g.   قُلْتُ كَيْتَ ذَيْتَ   or   قُلْتُ كَيْتَ وَذَيْتَ   I said such and such.

   e.g.   فَعَلْتُ كَيْتَ ذَيْتَ   or   فَعَلْتُ كَيْتَ وَذَيْتَ   I did such and such.

Section 2.4.8

<u>اَلْمُرَكَّبُ الْبِنَائِيُّ</u> – Numerical phrase

This has been discussed earlier. Please, refer to section 1.4.3.

Section 2.5

أَقْسَامُ اَلْأَسْمَاءِ الْمُعْرَبَةِ – Types of declinable *isms*

These are of two types:

1. <u>مُنْصَرِفٌ</u>

   <u>Definition:</u> It is an إِسْمٌ which does **not** have two causes from amongst the nine causes that prevent declension (أَسْبَابُ مَنْعِ الصَّرْفِ) **or** one such cause, which is equivalent to two.

   - It accepts all *harakaat* as well as *tanween*.

2. <u>غَيْرُ مُنْصَرِفٍ</u>

   <u>Definition:</u> It is an إِسْمٌ which has two causes from amongst the nine causes that prevent declension (أَسْبَابُ مَنْعِ الصَّرْفِ) **or** one such cause which is equivalent to two.

   - Such an *ism* does not accept a *kasrah* and never gets a *tanween*. In حَالَةُ الْجَرِّ, it gets a *fathah* in place of a *kasrah*.

<u>أَسْبَابُ مَنْعِ الصَّرْفِ</u> [23]

There are nine reasons/causes which prevent *i'raab* changes. Each one of these has its own conditions, which must exist for it to be a cause. The nine causes are as follows:

5. عُجْمَةٌ	4. تَأْنِيثٌ	3. عَلَمٌ	2. وَصْفٌ	1. عَدْلٌ
	9. جَمْعُ مُنْتَهَى الْجُمُوعِ	8. وَزْنُ فِعْلٍ	7. أَلِفٌ وَنُونٌ زَائِدَتَانِ	6. تَرْكِيبٌ

1. <u>عَدْلٌ</u>: It refers to the case when an إِسْمٌ gives up its original form to assume a new form.

   عَدْلٌ is of two types:

   i. <u>عَدْلٌ تَحْقِيقِيٌّ</u>: It refers to the case when an إِسْمٌ has an original.

      e.g.   In the case of ثُلَاثَ (three and three together), the original is ثَلَاثَةً وَثَلَاثَةً.

   ii. <u>عَدْلٌ تَقْدِيرِيٌّ</u>: It refers to the case when it is assumed that an إِسْمٌ had an original because it is used as غَيْرُ مُنْصَرِفٍ by the Arabs.

      e.g.   The Arabs use عُمَرُ as غَيْرُ مُنْصَرِفٍ. However, there is only one apparent cause, عَلَمٌ. Therefore, in order to keep the grammar rule intact, it is assumed that the second cause is عَدْلٌ and the original for عُمَرُ was عَامِرٌ.

---

[23] This discussion is based upon *Hidayat al-Nahw*. It is presented in an entirely different manner in *al-Nahw al-Wadih*. See *al-Nahw al-Wadih, Ibdtida'iyyah*, vol. 3, 125-133.

2. صِفَةٌ/وَصْفٌ: There can be two cases when an اِسْمٌ which is a صِفَةٌ would be *ghayr munsarif*.[24] These are as follows:

    i.   The صِفَةٌ was originally devised to give a descriptive (وَصْفِيٌّ) meaning. If such a صِفَةٌ is on the *wazn* of (أَفْعَل), and does not accept *taa* for its مُؤَنَّثٌ, it will be *ghayr munsarif*.

        e.g.   أَحْمَرُ   red   أَخْضَرُ   green

    ii.   The صِفَةٌ has أَلِفٌ وَ نُوْنٌ زَائِدَتَانِ. Its conditions are given below in (7).

3. عَلَمٌ: It refers to the case when an اِسْمٌ is a proper noun (name of a person, place or thing).

        e.g.   فَاطِمَةُ   female name

                حَضَرَمَوْتُ   name of a region in Yemen

4. تَأْنِيْثٌ: It refers to the case when an اِسْمٌ is a feminine proper noun (عَلَمٌ) with one of the following characteristics:

    i.   It ends with a round ة. For example,   طَلْحَةُ[25]   مَكَّةُ

    ii.   It does not end with a round ة and has more then three letters. For example, زَيْنَبُ.

    iii.   It is a non-Arabic three-letter word and the middle letter is سَاكِنٌ. For example, مِصْرُ.

Note:

    ▪   All *isms* ending in (اء) اَلْأَلِفُ الْمَمْدُودَةُ or (ىٰ) اَلْأَلِفُ الْمَقْصُوْرَةُ are feminine.

        e.g.   حُبْلَى   pregnant

                حَمْرَاءُ   red

    ▪   Presence of (اء) اَلْأَلِفُ الْمَمْدُودَةُ or (ىٰ) اَلْأَلِفُ الْمَقْصُوْرَةُ is **equivalent to two reasons**.

5. عُجْمَةٌ: It refers to the case when a word which is a proper noun (عَلَمٌ) in a non-Arabic language, has either

    ▪   more than three letters   e.g.   إِبْرَاهِيْمُ

        or

    ▪   has three letters and the middle letter is مُتَحَرِّكٌ.   e.g.   شَتَرُ (name of a fort)

        –   Thus, نُوْحٌ is *munsarif* because its middle letter is not مُتَحَرِّكٌ.

---

[24] *Sharh ibn ʿAqil*, vol. 3, 322-324.

[25] Even though طَلْحَةُ is a masculine proper noun, it is considered a feminine noun because of the presence of a round ة. For more discussion on the subject, see Section 3.4.

<u>Note</u>: The difference between نُوحٌ and مِصْرُ is that مِصْرُ is a feminine *ism* because of it being the name of a country, while نُوحٌ is not a feminine *ism*. Thus, مِصْرُ is *ghayr munsarif* because of تَأْنِيثٌ and عَلَمٌ, while نُوحٌ is *munsarif* because it only has عَلَمٌ. عُجْمَةٌ does not apply to either.

6. <u>تَرْكِيبٌ</u>: It refers to the case when a word is a combination of two words. This word must be a proper noun (عَلَمٌ).

    e.g.   بَعْلَبَكُّ   name of a city in Lebanon

            حَضَرَمَوْتُ   name of a region in Yemen

7. <u>أَلِفٌ وَنُونٌ زَائِدَتَانِ</u>: It refers to the case when an اِسْمٌ ends with an أَلِفٌ and نُونٌ (ـَانِ) and one of the following is true:

    i.   The أَلِفٌ and نُونٌ appear at the end of a proper noun (عَلَمٌ).

        e.g.   عُثْمَانُ   عِمْرَانُ

        <u>Note</u>: Thus, the word سَعْدَانٌ (grass) is not *ghayr munsarif* because it is not a proper noun.

    ii.   The أَلِفٌ and نُونٌ appear at the end of such a صِفَةٌ whose feminine is <u>not</u> on the وَزْنٌ of فَعْلَانَةٌ.

        e.g. سَكْرَانُ[26] intoxicated   عَطْشَانُ[27] thirsty

        Their feminines are <u>not</u> on the وَزْنٌ of فَعْلَانَةٌ.

        <u>Note</u>: Thus, the word نَدْمَانٌ is not *ghayr munsarif* because its feminine (نَدْمَانَةٌ) is on the *wazn* of فَعْلَانَةٌ.

- If the أَلِفٌ and نُونٌ are not extra or added (i.e. not زَائِدَتَانِ) but are part of the original letters of the word, then it will not be *ghayr munsarif*. For example, شَيْطَانٌ.

---

[26] سَكْرَانُ is mainly used as *ghayr munsarif* (without *tanween*), and is sometimes used as *munsarif* (with *tanween*). The reason is that it has two feminines. The main feminine is سَكْرَى, which requires that the masculine be *ghayr munsarif* (سَكْرَانُ). However, in the dialect of Banu Asad, the feminine is سَكْرَانَةٌ. This requires that the masculine be *munsarif* (سَكْرَانٌ). See E. W. Lane, *An Arabic-English Lexicon*, (Beirut: Librairie du Liban, 1968), book I, part 4, 1391.

[27] عَطْشَان is interchangeably used as *munsarif* (with *tanween*) and *ghayr munsarif* (without *tanween*). The reason is that it has two feminines. One is عَطْشَى, and the other is عَطْشَانَةٌ. Considering the first, it becomes *ghayr munsarif* (عَطْشَانُ); and considering the second, it becomes *munsarif* (عَطْشَانٌ). See Lane, book I, part 5, 2079.

8. وَزْنُ فِعْلٍ: It refers to the case when a proper noun (عَلَمٌ) is on the *wazn* of a فِعْلٌ or when a صِفَةٌ is on the *wazn* of أَفْعَلَ.

> e.g.   لَسْتَ بِأَسْبَقَ مِنْ أَحْمَدَ   You are not more advanced/ahead than Ahmad.
>
> Here, أَحْمَدَ is an عَلَمٌ and is on the *wazn* of the *fi'l* أَفْعَلُ , and أَسْبَقَ is a صِفَةٌ and is on the *wazn* of the verb أَفْعَلَ. Therefore, these two are *ghayr munsarif*.

> e.g.   جَاءَ يَزِيدُ   Yazeed came.
>
> Here, يَزِيدُ is an عَلَمٌ and is on the *wazn* of the *fi'l* يَفْعِلُ.

9. جَمْعُ مُنْتَهَى الْجُمُوْع: It is a plural which has, after the أَلِفُ الْجَمْع (*alif* of plural), one of the following:

> i. two مُتَحَرِّك letters.   e.g. مَسَاجِدُ mosques
>
> ii. one مُشَدَّد letter.   e.g. دَوَابُّ animals
>
> iii. three letters, the middle letter being سَاكِنٌ.   e.g. مَفَاتِيْحُ keys

Note:

- If any of the above words ends with a round ة, it will not be *ghayr munsarif*.

  e.g.   صَيَاقِلَةٌ   polishers

- جَمْعُ مُنْتَهَى الْجُمُوْع is **equivalent to two reasons/causes.**

General Note: A *ghayr munsarif ism* **will** get a *kasrah* in حَالَةُ الْجَرِّ in the following cases:

- when it is مُضَافٌ.   e.g. صَلَّيْتُ فِي مَسَاجِدِهِمْ   I prayed in their mosques.
- when it has ال before it.   e.g. ذَهَبْتُ إِلَى الْمَقَابِرِ   I went to the graves.

EXERCISES

1. Mention with reason why the following words are *munsarif* or *ghayr munsarif*.

i. زفر [28]	v. صحراء
ii. شيطان	vi. مصابيح
iii. أسود	vii. يزيد
iv. أساتذة	viii. غضبان [29]

---

[28] This is the name of a major Hanafi Imam. It is non-Arabic in origin and is pronounced with a *dammah* on the first letter and a *fathah* on the second letter.

[29] Its main feminine is غَضْىٰ. In the dialect of Banu Asad, its feminine is غَضْبَانَةٌ. See Lane, book I, part 6, 2265.

2. Translate, fill in the *i'raab* and point out with reason the words which are *ghayr munsarif*.

i. مررت بعمر

ii. ذهب أحمد مع زينب إلى مكة

iii. لا تسئلوا عن أشياء...الآية

iv. سقيت ولدا عطشان

v. يا أهل يثرب...الآية

vi. مررت بمساجد

vii. شهر رمضان الذى أنزل فيه القرآن...الآية

viii. إن الله اصطفى أُدم ونوحا وأُل إبرهيم وأُل عمران على العلمين (القرآن)

57

Section 2.6

إِعْرَابُ أَقْسَامِ الْأَسْمَاءِ الْمُعْرَبَةِ – *I'raab* of the various types of *mu'rab isms*

We begin this section by defining some terms. Then, we will outline the *i'raab* of each of the various types of *mu'rab isms*.

اَلْاِسْمُ الصَّحِيْحُ: It is an اِسْمٌ which does not end with any of the حُرُوْفُ الْعِلَّةِ (و – ا – ي).

e.g.   رَجُلٌ   man

اَلْاِسْمُ الْقَائِمِ مَقَامَ الصَّحِيْحِ: It is an اِسْمٌ which ends with a و or ي preceded by a سُكُوْنٌ.

e.g.   دَلْوٌ   bucket   ظَبْيٌ   deer

اَلْأَسْمَاءُ السِّتَّةُ الْمُكَبَّرَةُ: These are six *isms* which are not in their diminutive form (مُصَغَّر). These are as follows:

أَبٌ	father	فَمٌ	mouth
أَخٌ	brother	هَنٌ	something insignificant
حَمٌ	brother-in-law	ذُوْ (plural: أُولُوْ)	someone who possesses something

اَلْاِسْمُ الْمَقْصُوْرُ: It is an اِسْمٌ which ends with an اَلْأَلِفُ الْمَقْصُوْرَةُ (ى).

e.g.   مُوْسَى

اَلْاِسْمُ الْمَنْقُوْصُ: It is an اِسْمٌ which ends with a ي preceded by a *kasrah*.

e.g.   اَلْقَاضِيْ   the judge

<u>Note</u>: It should be remembered that the ي is visible in an اِسْمٌ مَنْقُوْصٌ when it is مَعْرِفَةٌ. When it is نَكِرَةٌ, the ي is not visible, e.g. اَلْقَاضِيْ becomes قَاضٍ. However, in حَالَةُ النَّصْبِ, it does become visible, e.g. رَأَيْتُ قَاضِيًا (I saw a judge).

Before we list the *i'raab* of each of the various types of *mu'rab isms* in a table, it would be useful to remember that a simple method of illustrating different *i'raab* is to make three sentences on the following pattern:

حَالَةُ الرَّفْعِ	حَالَةُ النَّصْبِ	حَالَةُ الْجَرِّ
جَاءَ زَيْدٌ	رَأَيْتُ زَيْدًا	مَرَرْتُ بِزَيْدٍ
Zayd came.	I saw Zayd.	I passed by Zayd.

In these three sentences, the word زَيْدٌ is displaying the different *i'raab* according to the changing state (حَالَة). Thus, it has a *dammah* in حَالَةُ الرَّفْعِ, and a *fathah* in حَالَةُ النَّصْبِ, and a *kasrah* in حَالَةُ الْجَرِّ.

Table 2.11
إِعْرَابُ أَقْسَامِ الْأَسْمَاءِ الْمُعْرَبَةِ

Ism Type	حَالَةُ الرَّفْعِ	حَالَةُ النَّصْبِ	حَالَةُ الْجَرِّ	Examples for each state
اَلْمُفْرَدُ الْمُنْصَرِفُ الصَّحِيْحُ	ضَمَّةٌ	فَتْحَةٌ	كَسْرَةٌ	مَرَرْتُ بِزَيْدٍ — رَأَيْتُ زَيْدًا — جَاءَ زَيْدٌ
اَلْمُفْرَدُ الْقَائِمُ مَقَامَ الصَّحِيْحِ	ضَمَّةٌ	فَتْحَةٌ	كَسْرَةٌ	مَرَرْتُ بِظَبْيٍ — رَأَيْتُ ظَبْيًا — هَذَا ظَبْيٌ
اَلْجَمْعُ الْمُكَسَّرُ الْمُنْصَرِفُ	ضَمَّةٌ	فَتْحَةٌ	كَسْرَةٌ	قُلْتُ لِرِجَالٍ[30] — رَأَيْتُ رِجَالًا — هُمْ رِجَالٌ
غَيْرُ الْمُنْصَرِفِ	ضَمَّةٌ	فَتْحَةٌ	فَتْحَةٌ	مَرَرْتُ بِعُمَرَ — رَأَيْتُ عُمَرَ — جَاءَ عُمَرُ
اَلْأَسْمَاءُ السِّتَّةُ الْمُكَبَّرَةُ a. When مُضَافٌ to any ism besides the ي dameer.[31]	و	ا	ي	مَرَرْتُ بِأَبِيْكَ — رَأَيْتُ أَبَاكَ — جَاءَ أَبُوْكَ
b. When مُضَافٌ to the ي dameer.	hidden	hidden	hidden	مَرَرْتُ بِأَبِيْ — رَأَيْتُ أَبِيْ — جَاءَ أَبِيْ
c. when not مُضَافٌ	ضَمَّةٌ	فَتْحَةٌ	كَسْرَةٌ	مَرَرْتُ بِأَبٍ — رَأَيْتُ أَبًا — جَاءَ أَبٌّ
اَلْمُضَافُ إِلَى يَاءِ الْمُتَكَلِّمِ	hidden	hidden	hidden	مَرَرْتُ بِزَمِيْلِيْ — رَأَيْتُ زَمِيْلِيْ — جَاءَ زَمِيْلِيْ
اَلاِسْمُ الْمَقْصُوْرُ	hidden	hidden	hidden	مَرَرْتُ بِمُوْسَى — رَأَيْتُ مُوْسَى — جَاءَ مُوْسَى
اَلاِسْمُ الْمَنْقُوْصُ مَعْرِفَةٌ	hidden	فَتْحَةٌ	hidden	مَرَرْتُ بِالْقَاضِيْ — رَأَيْتُ الْقَاضِيَ — جَاءَ الْقَاضِيْ
اَلاِسْمُ الْمَنْقُوْصُ نَكِرَةٌ	hidden	فَتْحَةٌ	hidden	مَرَرْتُ بِقَاضٍ — رَأَيْتُ قَاضِيًا — جَاءَ قَاضٍ
اَلْمُثَنَّى اِثْنَانِ (masculine) اِثْنَتَانِ (feminine)	ـَانِ	ـَيْنِ	ـَيْنِ	مَرَرْتُ بِرَجُلَيْنِ — رَأَيْتُ رَجُلَيْنِ — جَاءَ رَجُلَانِ
اِثْنَانِ (masculine) اِثْنَتَانِ (feminine)	ـَانِ	ـَيْنِ	ـَيْنِ	مَرَرْتُ بِاثْنَيْنِ — رَأَيْتُ اثْنَيْنِ — جَاءَ اثْنَانِ
كِلَا (masculine) كِلْتَا (feminine) (مُضَافٌ إِلَى الضَّمِيْرِ)	ـَا	ـَيْ	ـَيْ	مَرَرْتُ بِكِلَيْهِمَا — رَأَيْتُ كِلَيْهِمَا — جَاءَ كِلَاهُمَا[32]

---

[30] I said to some men.

[31] The م of فَمٌ is dropped when it is مُضَافٌ to any noun besides the ي dameer. For example, it is dropped in the following hadith: ...مَا تَجْعَلُ فِيْ فِيْ امْرَأَتِكَ (Whatever you put in the mouth of your wife...)

[32] Both of them.

59

Table 2.11 – *Continued*

Ism Type	حَالَةُ الرَّفْعِ	حَالَةُ النَّصْبِ	حَالَةُ الْجَرِّ	Examples for each state		
جَمْعُ الْمُؤَنَّثِ السَّالِمُ	‑َاتٌ	‑َاتٍ	‑َاتٍ	هُنَّ مُسْلِمَاتٌ	رَأَيْتُ مُسْلِمَاتٍ	مَرَرْتُ بِمُسْلِمَاتٍ
جَمْعُ الْمُذَكَّرِ السَّالِمُ	‑ُونَ	‑ِينَ	‑ِينَ	جَاءَ مُسْلِمُونَ	رَأَيْتُ مُسْلِمِينَ	مَرَرْتُ بِمُسْلِمِينَ
عِشْرُونَ إِلَى تِسْعُونَ – سِنُونَ	‑ُونَ	‑ِينَ	‑ِينَ	جَاءَ عِشْرُونَ رَجُلاً	رَأَيْتُ عِشْرِينَ رَجُلاً	مَرَرْتُ بِعِشْرِينَ رَجُلاً
أُولُو (plural of ذُو)	‑ُو	‑ِي	‑ِي	جَاءَ أُولُو مَالٍ	رَأَيْتُ أُولِي مَالٍ	مَرَرْتُ بِأُولِي مَالٍ
جَمْعُ الْمُذَكَّرِ السَّالِمُ (مُضَافٌ إِلَى يَاءِ الْمُتَكَلِّمِ)	hidden	‑ِيَّ	‑ِيَّ	هُؤُلَاءِ مُسْلِمِيَّ[33]	رَأَيْتُ مُسْلِمِيَّ[34]	مَرَرْتُ بِمُسْلِمِيَّ

EXERCISE[35]

1. Translate, fill in the *i'raab* and identify which rule from among those given in Table 2.11, is applicable.

i. نجى الفتى من الغرق

ii. الاقتصاد سبيل الغنى

iii. نحترم القاضي

iv. ناديت العاملين

v. كان التلاميذ منتبهين

vi. هجم الثعلب على الدجاجات

vii. اغسل فاك بعد كل طعام

---

[33] مُسْلِمِيَّ was originally مُسْلِمُوْنَ. First, the ن was dropped because of إِضَافَةٌ. It became مُسْلِمُوْيَ. Then, the و was changed to a ي and the two were joined according to the following morphological (صَرْفِيّ) rule: "when a و and a ي appear together and the first is سَاكِنٌ, then the و is changed to a ي, and the two ي are joined (this is called إِدْغَامٌ), and the *dammah* before the و is changed into a *kasrah*." Thus, it became مُسْلِمِيَّ.

[34] مُسْلِمِيَّ was originally مُسْلِمِيْنَ. First, the ن was dropped because of إِضَافَةٌ. It became مُسْلِمِيْ يَ. Then, the two ي were joined (إِدْغَامٌ). Thus, it became مُسْلِمِيَّ.

[35] For more exercises, refer to *al-Nahw al-Wadih*, *Ibtida'iyyah*, vol. 2, 13-51 & 83-94.

CHAPTER 3
Further discussion of *isms*

Section 3.1
اَلْاِسْمُ الْمَنْسُوْبُ – Relative adjective

<u>Definition:</u> It is that اِسْمٌ which shows something or someone to be related to it.

e.g.	بَغْدَادِيٌّ	someone or something from Baghdad
	صَرْفِيٌّ	an expert in morphology
	نَحْوِيٌّ	an expert in Arabic grammar
	هِنْدِيٌّ	someone or something from India

<u>Rules for creating اَلْاِسْمُ الْمَنْسُوْبُ:</u>

To show this relation, a يّ (يَاءُ النِّسْبَةِ الْمُشَدَّدَةُ) preceded by a *kasrah* is added at the end of the *ism* after affecting the following changes, if needed:

1. If a three-letter or a four-letter اِسْمٌ ends with an اَلْأَلِفُ الْمَقْصُوْرَةُ (ىٰ), then اَلْأَلِفُ الْمَقْصُوْرَةُ (ىٰ) should be changed to a و.

    e.g.   عِيْسَىٰ   becomes   عِيْسَوِيٌّ

    <u>Note:</u> In the case of a five-letter اِسْمٌ, the اَلْأَلِفُ الْمَقْصُوْرَةُ (ىٰ) should be dropped.

    e.g.   مُصْطَفَىٰ   becomes   مُصْطَفِيٌّ

2. If an اِسْمٌ ends with an اَلْأَلِفُ الْمَمْدُوْدَةُ (اء), then the ء should be changed to a و.

    e.g.   سَمَاءٌ   becomes   سَمَاوِيٌّ

3. That اِسْمٌ which already ends with a ي does not require يَاءُ النِّسْبَةِ.

    e.g.   شَافِعِيٌّ   would remain as is.

4. The round ة at the end of an اِسْمٌ should be dropped.

    e.g.   مَكَّةُ   becomes   مَكِّيٌّ   فَاطِمَةُ   becomes   فَاطِمِيٌّ

5. The round ة and ي of an اِسْمٌ which appears on the وَزْنٌ of فَعِيْلَةٌ and فُعَيْلَةٌ should be dropped.

    e.g.   مَدِيْنَةٌ   becomes   مَدَنِيٌّ   جُهَيْنَةُ   becomes   جُهَنِيٌّ

6. In case of the اِسْمٌ which appears on the وَزْنٌ of فَعِيْلٌ and ends with a ي, the first ي should be changed to a و preceded by a *fathah*, and the second ي should be dropped.

    e.g.   عَلِيٌّ (عَلِيْيٌ)   becomes   عَلَوِيٌّ

7. If the fourth letter of an اِسْمٌ is a ي preceded by a *kasrah*, then the ي can be dropped or it can be changed to a و.

    e.g.   دِهْلِيْ   becomes   دِهْلِيٌّ   or   دِهْلَوِيٌّ

8. If an original letter from the end of an اِسْمٌ was dropped, it should first be brought back, and then, the اِسْمٌ مَنْسُوْبٌ should be made.

    e.g.   أَبٌ (originally أَبَوٌ)   becomes   أَبَوِيٌّ
            أَخٌ (originally أَخَوٌ)   becomes   أَخَوِيٌّ
            دَمٌ (originally دَمَوٌ)   becomes   دَمَوِيٌّ

9. Some words do not follow any particular rule. They are based on usage.

    e.g.   نُوْرٌ   becomes   نُوْرَانِيٌّ   حَقٌّ   becomes   حَقَّانِيٌّ

EXERCISE

1. Form the اِسْمٌ مَنْسُوْبٌ from the following words.

    i. نَبِي   iv. مُوْسٰى

    ii. مصر   v. كوفة

    iii. بيضاء

Section 3.2
اَلْاِسْمُ التَّصْغِيرُ – Diminutive *ism*

<u>Definition:</u> It is an *ism* which is used to express the diminutive form of an *ism*. Sometimes, the purpose is to show affection or contempt.

<u>Rules:</u>

1. A three-letter *ism* would come on the *wazn* of فُعَيْلٌ (or فُعَيْلَةٌ for feminine).

    e.g.   رَجُلٌ   becomes   رُجَيْلٌ (a little man)

                 عَبْدٌ   becomes   عُبَيْدٌ (a little slave)

2. A four-letter *ism* would come on the *wazn* of فُعَيْعِلٌ.

    e.g.   جَعْفَرٌ   becomes   جُعَيْفِرٌ

3. A five-letter *ism* without a و, ا or ي as the fourth, would also come on the *wazn* of فُعَيْعِلٌ. The fifth letter would be dropped.

    e.g.   سَفَرْجَلٌ (name of a plant)   becomes   سُفَيْرِجٌ

    A five-letter *ism* having a و, ا or ي as the fourth letter, would come on the scale of فُعَيْعِيلٌ.

    e.g.   قِرْطَاسٌ (paper)   becomes   قُرَيْطِيسٌ

<u>Notes:</u>

1. In the diminutive form, the hidden ة of a مُؤَنَّثٌ سَمَاعِيٌّ becomes apparent.

    e.g.   شَمْسٌ   becomes   شُمَيْسَةٌ

2. In the diminutive form, the last letter of an *ism* which has been dropped becomes apparent.

    e.g.   اِبْنٌ (originally بَنْوٌ)   becomes   بُنَيٌّ

    (بُنَيٌّ was originally بُنَيْوٌ, and underwent a morphological process to become بُنَيٌّ)

EXERCISE

1. Form the diminutive *ism* from the following words.

    i. عقرب   iv. كلب

    ii. سلطان   v. أرض

    iii. عصفور   vi. قمر

Section 3.3

اَلْمَعْرِفَةُ وَالنَّكِرَةُ – Definite and indefinite *isms*

اَلنَّكِرَةُ (indefinite *ism*): It is an اِسْمٌ which denotes something unspecified.

e.g.   رَجُلٌ   **a** man

اَلْمَعْرِفَةُ (definite *ism*): It is an اِسْمٌ which denotes something specific. There are seven types of مَعْرِفَةٌ.

1. ضَمِيرٌ : It is a personal pronoun. It has been discussed earlier in Section 2.4.1.

2. عَلَمٌ : It is a proper noun, i.e. the name of a specific person, place or thing.

   e.g.   زَيْدٌ   مَكَّةُ   زَمْزَمُ

3. اِسْمُ الْإِشَارَةِ : It is the demonstrative اِسْمٌ. It has been discussed earlier in section 2.4.3.

4. اَلْاِسْمُ الْمَوْصُولُ : It is the relative pronoun. It has been discussed earlier in Section 2.4.2.

5. اَلْمُعَرِّفُ بِاللَّام : It is an اِسْمٌ which has ال (definite particle) at the beginning.

   e.g.   اَلرَّجُلُ   **the** man

6. That indefinite *ism* (نَكِرَةٌ) which is *mudaaf* to any of the above five definite *isms*.

   e.g.   كِتَابُكَ   كِتَابُ زَيْدٍ

   كِتَابُ الَّذِيْ   كِتَابُ هٰذَا الرَّجُلِ

   كِتَابُ الرَّجُلِ

7. اَلْمُنَادَى: It is the vocative اِسْمٌ, i.e. an اِسْمٌ which appears after a حَرْفُ نِدَاءٍ.

   e.g.   يَا رَجُلُ

EXERCISE

1. Which of the following words are *ma'rifah* (state what type) and which are *nakirah*.

   i. الفرس   v. مكة

   ii. نحن   vi. ذلك

   iii. سيارة الذي   vii. سمك

   iv. يا ولد   viii. سيف الرجل

Section 3.4

اَلِاسْمُ الْمُذَكَّرُ وَالْمُؤَنَّثُ – Masculine and feminine *ism*

اَلِاسْمُ الْمُذَكَّرُ - **Masculine *im*:** It is an اِسْمٌ which does not have any sign from amongst the signs of femininity (عَلَامَاتُ التَّأْنِيثِ).

اَلِاسْمُ الْمُؤَنَّثُ - **Feminine *ism*:** It is an اِسْمٌ which has a sign from amongst the signs of femininity. This sign could be apparent or hidden.

عَلَامَاتُ التَّأْنِيثِ: The signs of being feminine are of two types:

1. لَفْظِيٌّ (in words): It is a sign which is visible in words. These signs are of the following three types:

   - ة: This renders the word اَلِاسْمُ الْمُؤَنَّثُ even if the ة appears in a masculine proper noun. e.g. سَيَّارَةٌ طَلْحَةُ (a masculine proper noun)

   - اَلْأَلِفُ الْمَقْصُورَةُ (ى) e.g. صُغْرَى حُبْلَى

   - اَلْأَلِفُ الْمَمْدُودَةُ (اء) e.g. بَيْضَاءُ حَمْرَاءُ

   If a word has any of these three signs it will be اَلِاسْمُ الْمُؤَنَّثُ.

2. تَقْدِيرِيٌّ (assumed): It is a sign which is not visible in words and is assumed to exist. This is determined by looking at the diminutive form (تَصْغِيرٌ) of a particular word. This reveals the original letters of the word.

   e.g. أَرْضٌ The diminutive form is أُرَيْضَةٌ. Therefore, it is اَلِاسْمُ الْمُؤَنَّثُ.

   شَمْسٌ The diminutive form is شُمَيْسَةٌ. Therefore, it is اَلِاسْمُ الْمُؤَنَّثُ.

Based on the signs of femininity being لَفْظِيٌّ or تَقْدِيرِيٌّ, اَلِاسْمُ الْمُؤَنَّثُ is of two types:

1. اَلْمُؤَنَّثُ الْقِيَاسِيُّ (according to rule): It is a feminine اِسْمٌ which has a لَفْظِيٌّ sign of femininity.

2. اَلْمُؤَنَّثُ السَّمَاعِيُّ (according to usage): It is a feminine اِسْمٌ which has a تَقْدِيرِيٌّ sign of femininity.

In terms of ذَاتٌ (essence), اَلِاسْمُ الْمُؤَنَّثُ is of two types:

1. مُؤَنَّثٌ حَقِيقِيٌّ: It is a feminine اِسْمٌ which has an opposite masculine.

   e.g. اِمْرَأَةٌ (woman). Its masculine is رَجُلٌ (man).

2. مُؤَنَّثٌ لَفْظِيٌّ: It is a feminine اِسْمٌ which does not have an opposite masculine.

   e.g. ظُلْمَةٌ (darkness) عَيْنٌ (eye)

Notes:

1. The following are used as feminine (مُؤَنَّثٌ):

   a. Name of females.

   e.g. مَرْيَمُ   زَيْنَبُ

   b. Words denoting the feminine gender.

   e.g. أُمٌّ   أُخْتٌ

   c. Names of countries, cities, towns and tribes.

   e.g. مِصْرُ   قُرَيْشٌ

   d. Parts of the body found in pairs.

   e.g. أُذُنٌ   يَدٌّ

   Note: There are exceptions to the rule. خَدٌّ (cheek), حَاجِبٌ (eyebrow) etc. are masculine.

   e. Names of various types of winds.

   e.g. رِيْحٌ   صَرْصَرٌ

   f. Various names of *Jahannam* (hell).

   e.g. جَهَنَّمُ   سَقَرُ

   g. Letters of the alphabet (اَلْحُرُوْفُ الْهِجَائِيَّةُ) are generally used as مُؤَنَّثٌ. They can also be used as masculine.

   e.g. ا   ب   ت   ....

2. There are some words that Arabs use as feminine without regard to the presence or absence of signs of femininity. Examples include the following:

دَلْوٌ (bucket)	حَرْثٌ (tillage/field)	بِئْرٌ (well)
نَفْسٌ (self)	نَارٌ (fire)	دَارٌ (house)

Section 3.5
وَاحِدٌ وَتَثْنِيَةٌ وَجَمْعٌ – Singular, dual and plural

<u>وَاحِدٌ – **Singular:**</u> It is an *ism* which denotes one of something.

e.g.   رَجُلٌ   one man

<u>تَثْنِيَةٌ – **Dual:**</u> It is an *ism* which denotes two of something. It is formed by placing at the end of a singular (وَاحِدٌ) one of the following:

- An أَلِفٌ preceded by a *fathah* and followed by a نُوْنٌ with a *kasrah* i.e. [ـَانِ] for حَالَةُ الرَّفْعِ.
  (أَلِفٌ مَا قَبْلَهَا مَفْتُوحٌ وَبَعْدَهَا نُوْنٌ مَكْسُورَةٌ)

  e.g.   رَجُلَانِ   two men

- A يَاءٌ preceded by a *fathah* and followed by a نُوْنٌ with a *kasrah* i.e. [ـَيْنِ] for حَالَةُ النَّصْبِ
  (يَاءٌ مَا قَبْلَهَا مَفْتُوحٌ وَبَعْدَهَا نُوْنٌ مَكْسُورَةٌ). وَالْجَرِّ

  e.g.   رَجُلَيْنِ   two men

<u>جَمْعٌ – **Plural:**</u> It is an *ism* which denotes more than two of something.

e.g.   رِجَالٌ   men

<u>Note:</u> The نُوْنٌ of تَثْنِيَةٌ and جَمْعٌ is dropped in case of إِضَافَةٌ.

e.g.   قَلَمَا زَيْدٍ   (Originally قَلَمَانِ زَيْدٍ but the نُوْنٌ was dropped due to إِضَافَةٌ.)

         فَرَسَا رَجُلٍ   (Originally فَرَسَانِ رَجُلٍ but the نُوْنٌ was dropped due to إِضَافَةٌ.)

         مُسْلِمُوْ مِصْرَ   (Originally مُسْلِمُوْنَ مِصْرَ but the نُوْنٌ was dropped due to إِضَافَةٌ.)

         طَالِبُوْ عِلْمٍ   (Originally طَالِبُوْنَ عِلْمٍ but the نُوْنٌ was dropped due to إِضَافَةٌ.)

EXERCISE

1. Translate the following into Arabic.

   i. The boy's two bicycles.
   ii. The farmer's two servants.
   iii. Your parents came.
   iv. I saw your parents.
   v. The servants of *deen*.
   vi. The teachers of the school.

Section 3.6

أَقْسَامُ الْجَمْعِ – Types of plural

اَلْجَمْعُ السَّالِمُ – Sound plural: It is a plural whose صِيغَةٌ (letter sequence/form) of وَاحِدٌ does not change when its plural is made. In other words, the singular letter sequence does not break.

e.g.   مُسْلِمُوْنَ   (مُسْلِمٌ – singular)

There are two types of اَلْجَمْعُ السَّالِمُ:

1. جَمْعُ مُذَكَّرٍ سَالِمٌ – Masculine sound plural: It is formed by adding at the end of a singular (وَاحِدٌ) one of the following:

   - A وَاوٌ preceded by a *dammah* and followed by a نُوْنْ with a *fathah* i.e. [ـُوْنَ] for (وَاوٌ مَا قَبْلَهَا مَضْمُوْمٌ وَبَعْدَهَا نُوْنٌ مَفْتُوْحَةٌ). حَالَةُ الرَّفْعِ

     e.g.   مُسْلِمُوْنَ

   - A يَاءٌ preceded by a *kasrah* and followed by a نُوْنْ with a *fathah* i.e. [ـِيْنَ] for (يَاءٌ مَا قَبْلَهَا مَكْسُوْرٌ وَبَعْدَهَا نُوْنٌ مَفْتُوْحَةٌ). حَالَةُ النَّصْبِ وَالْجَرِّ

     e.g.   مُسْلِمِيْنَ

2. جَمْعُ مُؤَنَّثٍ سَالِمٌ – Feminine sound plural: It is formed by discarding the round ة and adding at the end of a singular one of the following:

   - An أَلِفٌ preceded by a *fathah* and followed by a *madmoom* long ت i.e. [ـَاتٌ] for (أَلِفٌ مَا قَبْلَهَا مَفْتُوْحٌ وَبَعْدَهَا تَاءٌ مَضْمُوْمَةٌ). حَالَةُ الرَّفْعِ

     e.g.   مُسْلِمَاتٌ

   - An أَلِفٌ preceded by a *fathah* and followed by a *maksoor* long ت i.e. [ـَاتِ] for (أَلِفٌ مَا قَبْلَهَا مَفْتُوْحٌ وَبَعْدَهَا تَاءٌ مَكْسُوْرَةٌ). حَالَةُ النَّصْبِ وَ الْجَرِّ

     e.g.   مُسْلِمَاتِ

اَلْجَمْعُ الْمُكَسَّرُ – Broken plural: It is a plural whose صِيغَةٌ (the singular letter sequence/form) of وَاحِدٌ changes when its plural is made. In other words, the singular letter sequence breaks.

e.g.   رِجَالٌ   (رَجُلٌ – singular)

68

<u>جَمْعُ قِلَّةٍ</u> – **Restricted Plural:** It is a plural which denotes a number from three to ten. It has four common أَوْزَانٌ.

Table 3.1

أَوْزَانُ جَمْعِ قِلَّةٍ

Wazn	Examples		
	Singular	Meaning	Plural
أَفْعُلٌ	نَفْسٌ	self	أَنْفُسٌ
أَفْعَالٌ	قَوْلٌ	statement	أَقْوَالٌ
أَفْعِلَةٌ	طَعَامٌ	food	أَطْعِمَةٌ
فِعْلَةٌ	غُلَامٌ	boy	غِلْمَةٌ

<u>Note:</u> The masculine and feminine sound plural, which is <u>not</u> preceded by an ال is also considered جَمْعُ قِلَّةٍ.

e.g.   عَاقِلَاتٌ   intelligent females   عَاقِلُونَ   intelligent males

<u>جَمْعُ كَثْرَةٍ</u> – **Unrestricted Plural:** It is a plural which denotes a number from three upwards. Some of the common أَوْزَانٌ are given below.

Table 3.2

أَوْزَانُ جَمْعِ كَثْرَةٍ

Wazn	Examples		
	Singular	Meaning	Plural
فِعَالٌ	عَبْدٌ	slave	عِبَادٌ
فُعَلَاءُ	عَلِيمٌ	knowledgeable	عُلَمَاءُ
أَفْعِلَاءُ	نَبِيٌّ	prophet	أَنْبِيَاءُ
فُعُلٌ	رَسُولٌ	messenger	رُسُلٌ
فُعُولٌ	نَجْمٌ	star	نُجُومٌ
فُعَّالٌ	خَادِمٌ	servant	خُدَّامٌ
فَعْلَى	مَرِيضٌ	patient	مَرْضَى
فَعَلَةٌ	طَالِبٌ	student	طَلَبَةٌ
فِعَلٌ	فِرْقَةٌ	group/sect	فِرَقٌ
فِعْلَانٌ	غُلَامٌ	boy	غِلْمَانٌ

69

The masculine and feminine sound plural which is preceded by an ال is also considered as جَمْعُ كَثْرَةٍ.

e.g. ٱلْمُسْلِمَاتُ   ٱلْمُسْلِمُوْنَ

جَمْعُ الْجَمْعِ – Plural of a plural: It is the plural of a plural. Sometimes, it appears on the *wazn* of مُنْتَهَى الْجُمُوعِ and sometimes on the *wazn* of ٱلْجَمْعُ السَّالِمُ. Not every plural has a plural. Some examples of plurals which have a plural are given below.

Table 3.3
أَمْثَالُ جَمْعِ الْجَمْعِ

Singular	Meaning	Plural	Plural of plural
نِعْمَةٌ	blessing	أَنْعُمٌ	أَنَاعِمُ
ظُفْرٌ	nail	أَظَافِرُ	أَظَافِيْرُ
بَيْتٌ	house	بُيُوْتٌ	بُيُوْتَاتٌ
فَاضِلٌ	well-qualified	أَفَاضِلُ	أَفَاضِلُوْنَ

مُنْتَهَى الْجُمُوْعِ: It is a plural which has after the أَلِفُ الْجَمْعِ (*alif* of plural), one of the following:

- two مُتَحَرِّكٌ letters.   e.g.   مَسَاجِدُ
- one مُشَدَّدٌ letter.   e.g.   دَوَابُّ (the original being دَوَابِبُ)
- three letters, the middle one being سَاكِنٌ.   e.g.   مَفَاتِيْحُ

Some of the common *wazns* of مُنْتَهَى الْجُمُوعِ are given below:

Table 3.4
أَوْزَانُ مُنْتَهَى الْجُمُوعِ

Wazn	Examples		
	Singular	Meaning	Plural
مَفَاعِلُ	مَسْجِدٌ	mosque	مَسَاجِدُ
مَفَاعِيْلُ	مِفْتَاحٌ	key	مَفَاتِيْحُ
فَوَاعِلُ	قَاعِدَةٌ	rule/maxim	قَوَاعِدُ
فَعَائِلُ	رِسَالَةٌ	message/letter	رَسَائِلُ
أَفَاعِلُ	أَكْبَرُ	elder	أَكَابِرُ

70

اِسْمُ الْجَمْعِ – **Collective** *ism*:[36] It is a singular اِسْمٌ which conveys a plural meaning. Generally, it does not have a singular from the same word.

e.g.   قَوْمٌ   nation

          رَهْطٌ   group

<u>Note:</u>

1. These words have plurals.

e.g.   قَوْمٌ ⟶ أَقْوَامٌ   رَهْطٌ ⟶ أَرْهَاطٌ

2. In usage, if the <u>word</u> is considered, it will be used as a singular اِسْمٌ.

e.g.   اَلْقَوْمُ حَاضِرٌ   The people are present.

If its <u>meaning</u> is considered (as is commonly done), it will be used as a plural اِسْمٌ.

e.g.   قَوْمٌ صَالِحُوْنَ   righteous people

<u>Notes:</u>

1. Some plurals do not have the same root letters as their singulars.

e.g.   اِمْرَأَةٌ (woman) ⟶ نِسَاءٌ

        ذُوْ (the one who possesses something) ⟶ أُولُوْ

2. Some plurals are not according to rule (خِلَافُ الْقِيَاسِ).

e.g.   أُمٌّ (mother) ⟶ أُمَّهَاتٌ

        فَمٌ (mouth) ⟶ أَفْوَاهٌ

        مَاءٌ (water) ⟶ مِيَاهٌ

        إِنْسَانٌ (human being) ⟶ أُنَاسٌ

        شَاةٌ (goat/sheep) ⟶ شِيَاهٌ

اِسْمُ الْجِنْسِ – **Generic** *ism*:[37] It is an اِسْمٌ which is devised for an essence (مَاهِيَة). Because of that, it refers to an entire genus (category/class). Generally, its singular has a (ة). For example,

شَجَرٌ refers to trees. Its singular is شَجَرَةٌ (a tree).

نَخْلٌ refers to date-palm trees. Its singular is نَخْلَةٌ (a date-palm tree).

---

[36] For more details, please refer to 'Abd al-Ghaniyy al-Daqr, *Mu'jam al-Qawa'id al-'Arabiyyah fi al-Nahw wa al-Tasreef* (Damascus: Dar al-Qalam, 1986), 36.

[37] For more details, please refer to *Mu'jam al-Qawa'id al-'Arabiyyah*, 36.

EXERCISE

1. What type of plurals are the following?

i. صائمات		ii. جيش		iii. أكلب	
iv. مصابيح		v. بلاد		vi. كتب	
vii. صائمون		viii. إبل		ix. غنم	

Section 3.7

اَلْمَرْفُوعَاتُ - Words that are always *marfoo'*

There are eight words that are always in the state of رَفْعٌ. These are as follows:

1. فَاعِلٌ	2. نَائِبُ الْفَاعِلِ	3. مُبْتَدَأٌ	4. خَبَرٌ	5. خَبَرُ إِنَّ وَأَخَوَاتِهَا
6. اِسْمُ كَانَ وَأَخَوَاتِهَا		7. اِسْمُ مَا وَلَا الْمُشَبَّهَتَيْنِ بِلَيْسَ		8. خَبَرُ لَا الَّتِي لِنَفْيِ الْجِنْسِ

Some of these have been discussed before. مُبْتَدَأٌ (subject) and خَبَرٌ (predicate) were discussed in Section 1.4.1, خَبَرُ إِنَّ وَأَخَوَاتِهَا was discussed in Section 1.8, and اِسْمُ كَانَ وَأَخَوَاتِهَا was discussed in Section 1.9. We discuss the rest below.

Section 3.7.1

فَاعِلٌ – Subject/Doer

<u>Definition:</u> It is the doer of the action or of the meaning contained in the فِعْلٌ.

- The فَاعِلٌ can either be a personal pronoun or an اِسْمٌ ظَاهِرٌ (i.e. visible in words after the فِعْلٌ). We have discussed personal pronouns before in Section 2.4.1. Now, we will discuss what the فِعْلٌ should be for various types of فَاعِلٌ.

Table 3.5

اِسْتِعْمَالُ الْفِعْلِ حَسْبَ الْفَاعِلِ

If the فَاعِلٌ is	Then the فِعْلٌ will be	Example
1. ظَاهِرٌ مُؤَنَّثٌ حَقِيقِيٌّ and there is no word between the فِعْلٌ and the فَاعِلٌ.	وَاحِدٌ مُؤَنَّثٌ	قَامَتْ عَائِشَةُ
2. ضَمِيرٌ مُؤَنَّثٌ	مُؤَنَّثٌ and its singularity, duality, or plurality will be according to the preceding *ism* that it refers to.	اَلْمُعَلِّمَةُ نَصَرَتْ - اَلْمُعَلِّمَتَانِ نَصَرَتَا - اَلْمُعَلِّمَاتُ نَصَرْنَ
3. ظَاهِرٌ مُؤَنَّثٌ حَقِيقِيٌّ and there is a word between the فِعْلٌ and the فَاعِلٌ.	وَاحِدٌ مُؤَنَّثٌ or وَاحِدٌ مُذَكَّرٌ	قَرَأَ الْيَوْمَ عَائِشَةُ or قَرَأَتِ الْيَوْمَ عَائِشَةُ
4. ظَاهِرٌ مُؤَنَّثٌ غَيْرُ حَقِيقِيٍّ	وَاحِدٌ مُؤَنَّثٌ or وَاحِدٌ مُذَكَّرٌ	طَلَعَتِ الشَّمْسُ or طَلَعَ الشَّمْسُ
5. ظَاهِرٌ جَمْعٌ مُكَسَّرٌ	وَاحِدٌ مُؤَنَّثٌ or وَاحِدٌ مُذَكَّرٌ	قَالَتِ الرِّجَالُ or قَالَ الرِّجَالُ

Table 3.5 – *Continued*

If the فَاعِلٌ is	Then the فِعْلٌ will be	Example
6. any اِسْمٌ ظَاهِرٌ beside the above five categories	وَاحِدٌ corresponding in gender	ضَرَبَ الرَّجُلُ – ضَرَبَ الرَّجُلَانِ – ضَرَبَ الرِّجَالُ
7. ضَمِيرٌ مُذَكَّرٌ	مُذَكَّرٌ and its singularity, duality, or plurality will be according to the preceding اِسْمٌ that it refers to	اَلْخَادِمُ ذَهَبَ – اَلْخَادِمَانِ ذَهَبَا – اَلْخَادِمُوْنَ ذَهَبُوْا
8. ضَمِيرٌ that referes to جَمْعٌ مُكَسَّرٍ	وَاحِدٌ مُؤَنَّثٌ or جَمْعٌ مُذَكَّرٌ	اَلرِّجَالُ قَامَتْ or اَلرِّجَالُ قَامُوْا

EXERCISE

1. Fill in a suitable فِعْلٌ in the spaces below.

i. الولدان _____   ii. الطلابُ _____/_____

iii. _____ النساء   iv. السفينة _____/_____

v. _____/_____ الأطفال   vi. اليوم امرأةٌ _____/_____

74

Section 3.7.2
فَاعِلٌ Substitute of – مَفْعُولُ مَا لَمْ يُسَمَّ فَاعِلُهُ / نَائِبُ الْفَاعِلِ

Definition: It is an اِسْمٌ which is the فَاعِلٌ of a فِعْلٌ مَجْهُولٌ (passive voice). The original فَاعِلٌ is dropped and the مَفْعُولٌ بِهِ subsitutes it. This is why, it is called نَائِبُ الْفَاعِلِ (substitute of فَاعِلٌ) or مَفْعُولُ مَا لَمْ يُسَمَّ فَاعِلُهُ (the مَفْعُولٌ of such a فِعْلٌ whose فَاعِلٌ is not mentioned).

e.g.   نُصِرَ زَيْدٌ   Zayd was helped. (The doer is not known/mentioned.)

The same فِعْلٌ – فَاعِلٌ usage rules apply as mentioned above in Table 3.5.

e.g.
1. نُصِرَتْ عَائِشَةُ
2. عَائِشَةُ نُصِرَتْ
3. نُصِرَ الْيَوْمَ عَائِشَةُ or نُصِرَتِ الْيَوْمَ عَائِشَةُ
4. رُئِيَ الشَّمْسُ or رُئِيَتِ الشَّمْسُ
5. ضُرِبَ الرِّجَالُ or ضُرِبَتِ الرِّجَالُ
6. ضُرِبَ الرَّجُلُ or ضُرِبَ الرَّجُلَانِ or ضُرِبَ الرِّجَالُ
7. اَلْخَادِمُ طُلِبَ or اَلْخَادِمَانِ طُلِبَا or اَلْخَادِمُونَ طُلِبُوا
8. اَلرِّجَالُ ضُرِبَتْ or اَلرِّجَالُ ضُرِبُوا

Sentence Analysis:

الْبَابُ	فُتِحَ	The door was opened.
نَائِبُ الْفَاعِلِ	فِعْلٌ مَجْهُولٌ	

EXERCISE

1. Convert the following to فِعْلٌ مَجْهُولٌ with its نَائِبُ الْفَاعِلِ.

    i. سرق اللص المال   iii. نعبد الله

    ii. فتح زيد الأبواب   iv. ذبح الرجل الشاة

2. Convert the following to مَفْعُولٌ – فَاعِلٌ – فِعْلٌ.

    i. تُحْلَبُ البقرة   iii. سُئِلَ المعلم

    ii. قُطِعَتِ الزهرة   iv. شُرِبَ اللبن

75

<u>Section 3.7.3</u>[38]

<u>اِسْمُ مَا وَلَا اَلْمُشَبَّهَتَيْنِ بِلَيْسَ – *Ism* of those مَا and لَا which are similar to لَيْسَ</u>

- It means that مَا and لَا have the same meaning and effect (عَمَلٌ) as لَيْسَ.

  e.g. مَا زَيْدٌ قَائِمًا   Zayd is not standing.

  لَا رَجُلٌ أَفْضَلَ مِنْكَ   No man is more virtuous than you.

- Like لَيْسَ, sometimes, an extra *baa'* (بَاءٌ زَائِدَةٌ) is added before the خَبَرٌ.

  e.g. مَا أَنَا بِقَارِئٍ   I am not a reader/I cannot read.

- The effect of مَا and لَا is cancelled if any of the following occurs:

  i.   When the خَبَرٌ appears before the اِسْمٌ.

  e.g. مَا قَائِمٌ زَيْدٌ   Zayd is not standing.

  ii. The word إِلَّا appears before the خَبَرٌ negating the negative meaning of مَا and لَا.

  e.g. مَا مُحَمَّدٌ إِلَّا رَسُولٌ   And Muhammad is not but a messenger./
         And Muhammad is only a messenger.
         [Allah bless him and give him peace]

  iii. If the اِسْمٌ and/or خَبَرٌ of لَا is not نَكِرَةٌ. (مَا can appear before a مَعْرِفَةٌ or a نَكِرَةٌ)

  e.g. لَا الْمَدِينَةُ كَبِيرَةٌ   The city is not big.

---

[38] For more details, examples and exercises, please refer to *al-Nahw al-Wadih, Thanawiyyah*, vol. 1, 95-102.

<u>Section 3.7.4</u>[39]

خَبَرُ لَا الَّتِي لِنَفْيِ الْجِنْسِ – The خَبَر of that لَا which negates an entire جِنْسٌ (category/class)

- لَا gives its اِسْم a single *fathah* and its خَبَر a *dammah* when the اِسْم and the خَبَر are نَكِرَةٌ.

  e.g. لَا رَجُلَ قَائِمٌ   No man is standing.

Table 3.6
Different forms of the *ism* of لَا and its *i'raab*

	If the اِسْم of لَا is	Then it will be	Explanation	Example
1.	شِبْهُ الْمُضَافِ [40] or مُضَافٌ	مَنْصُوبٌ		لَا خَادِمَ رَجُلٍ فِي الدَّارِ There is no servant of a man in the house. لَا سَاعِيًا خَيْرًا مَذْمُومٌ No one who attempts to do good is blameworthy.
2.	نَكِرَةٌ مُفْرَدَةٌ	مَبْنِيٌّ عَلَى الْفَتْحِ		لَا رَجُلَ فِي الدَّارِ There is no man in the house.
3.	مَعْرِفَةٌ	مَرْفُوعٌ	- The لَا has to be repeated with another مَعْرِفَةٌ. - The effect of لَا is cancelled.	لَا زَيْدٌ فِي الدَّارِ وَلَا عَمْرُو Neither is Zayd in the house nor 'Amr.
4.	نَكِرَةٌ with a word between it and لَا	مَرْفُوعٌ	- The لَا has to be repeated. - The effect of لَا is cancelled.	لَا فِيهَا رَجُلٌ وَلَا امْرَأَةٌ Neither is there a man in it nor a woman.
5.	لَا and نَكِرَةٌ repeated with no word between them	فَتْحُهُمَا رَفْعُهُمَا فَتْحُ الْأَوَّلِ وَنَصْبُ الثَّانِي فَتْحُ الْأَوَّلِ وَرَفْعُ الثَّانِي رَفْعُ الْأَوَّلِ وَفَتْحُ الثَّانِي		لَا حَوْلَ وَلَا قُوَّةَ [41] لَا حَوْلَ وَلَا قُوَّةٌ لَا حَوْلَ وَلَا قُوَّةَ لَا حَوْلَ وَلَا قُوَّةٌ لَا حَوْلٌ وَلَا قُوَّةَ

---

[39] For more details, examples and exercises, please refer to *al-Nahw al-Wadih*, *Thanawiyyah*, vol. 1, 118-122.

[40] It refers to the case when a word is connected to another word, which completes its meaning, in the same way that *mudaaf* and *mudaaf ilayhi* are connected to one another.

[41] There is no power (to do good) and there is no power (to stay away from evil) [except with Allah's help].

Note: The خَبَر of لَا may be omitted when the meaning is understood.

e.g.   لَا بَأْسَ   i.e.   لَا بَأْسَ عَلَيْكَ   There is no harm upon you. / No problem.

EXERCISE

1. Translate, fill in the *i'raab* and point out the rule which applies.

i.   لا خير فى مال البخيل لنفسه   v.   لا بكر فى الفصل ولا حسن

ii.   لا طالب علم فى الفصل   vi.   لا فى الفصل معلم ولا طالب

iii.   لا صاحب جُود مذموم   vii.   لا دار كتب فى المدينة

iv.   لا الرجل كريم ولا ابنه   viii.   لا فى الحديقة صبيان ولا بنات

78

Section 3.8

اَلْمَنْصُوبَاتُ – Words which are always *mansoob*[42]

1. مَفْعُوْلٌ بِهِ	7. اَلتَّمْيِيزُ / اَلتَّمْيِيزُ
2. مَفْعُوْلٌ مُطْلَقٌ	8. اِسْمُ إِنَّ وَأَخَوَاتِهَا
3. مَفْعُوْلٌ لَهُ	9. خَبَرُ مَا وَلَا اَلْمُشَبَّهَتَيْنِ بِلَيْسَ
4. مَفْعُوْلٌ مَعَهُ	10. اِسْمُ لَا اَلَّتِيْ لِنَفْيِ الْجِنْسِ
5. مَفْعُوْلٌ فِيْهِ	11. خَبَرُ كَانَ وَأَخَوَاتِهَا
6. اَلْحَالُ	12. اَلْمُسْتَثْنَى

known as اَلْمَفَاعِيْلُ الْخَمْسَةُ

Of these, 8, 9, 10 and 11 have been discussed before. Here, we will discuss the remaining.

Section 3.8.1

مَفْعُوْلٌ بِهِ – Object

<u>Definition:</u> It is that word on which the action of the فَاعِلٌ takes place.

e.g.	مَاءً	خَالِدٌ	شَرِبَ	Khalid drank water.
	مَفْعُوْلٌ بِهِ	فَاعِلٌ	فِعْلٌ	

- Sometimes, the فِعْلٌ governing the مَفْعُوْلٌ بِهِ is dropped as in the following:

  a. مُنَادَى (the one being called):[43]

e.g.	اِبْنَ زَيْدٍ	يَا	O son of Zayd!
	مُنَادَى (مَفْعُوْلٌ بِهِ)	حَرْفُ النِّدَاءِ	

  It was originally (أَدْعُوْ اِبْنَ زَيْدٍ). The *fi'l* أَدْعُوْ was dropped.

  <u>Note:</u>

  - The حَرْفُ النِّدَاءِ (vocative particle) substitutes the omitted فِعْلٌ.

    Some of the vocative particles are as follows:

أ	and	أَيْ	These are used when the مُنَادَى is near.
أَيَا	and	هَيَا	These are used when the مُنَادَى is far.
يَا			This is used for both (near and far).

---

[42] There are exceptions to the rule. *Mustathnaa*, for example, is not always *mansoob*. It is still mentioned under this category because most of the time, it is *mansoob*.

[43] For more details, examples and exercises, please refer to *al-Nahw al-Wadih, Ibtida'iyyah*, vol. 3, 120-124.

Table 3.7
Rules governing the *i'raab* of the مُنَادَى

If the مُنَادَى is	Then it will be	Example	
1. مُضَافٌ	مَنْصُوبٌ	يَا ابْنَ زَيْدٍ	O son of Zayd!
2. شَبِيهَةٌ بِالْمُضَافِ [44]	مَنْصُوبٌ	يَا قَارِءًا كِتَابًا	O reader of a book!
3. نَكِرَةٌ غَيْرُ مُعَيَّنَةٍ (Unspecified *nakirah*)	مَنْصُوبٌ	يَا رَجُلًا! خُذْ بِيَدِي	O man! Take my hand. (call of a blind man to **any** person for assisstance)
4. نَكِرَةٌ مُعَيَّنَةٌ (Specified *nakirah*)	مَرْفُوعٌ	يَا رَجُلُ	O man!
5. مَعْرِفَةٌ مُفْرَدَةٌ (Singular *ma'rifah*)	مَرْفُوعٌ	يَا زَيْدُ	O Zayd!
6. مُعَرَّفٌ بِ ال	مَرْفُوعٌ	أَيُّهَا (masculine) or أَيَّتُهَا (feminine) has to be added between the حَرْفُ النِّدَاءِ and مُنَادَى. يَا أَيَّتُهَا الْمَرْأَةُ O man! يَا أَيُّهَا الرَّجُلُ O woman!	

- تَرْخِيمٌ (abbreviation) is allowed in *munaadaa*.

  e.g. يَا مَالِكُ can become يَا مَالُ or يَا مَالِ

  يَا مَنْصُورُ can become يَا مَنْصُ

  <u>Note:</u> The last letter can be given a *dammah* or it can retain its original *harakah*.

b. <u>أَهْلًا وَ سَهْلًا</u>: This is said to one's guest for welcoming him/her.

Its original is أَتَيْتَ أَهْلًا وَوَطِئْتَ سَهْلًا, which means "You have come to your own people and have trampled comfortable ground." In other words, "you are welcome." Here two *fi'ls*, أَتَيْتَ and وَطِئْتَ have been dropped.

c. Sometimes, when warning someone, the فِعْلٌ governing the مَفْعُولٌ بِهِ is dropped due to context. Examples include the following:

- الطَّرِيْقَ الطَّرِيْقَ is used instead of اِتَّقِ الطَّرِيْقَ to give the same meaning, which is "Beware of the road!" Here, the *fi'l* اِتَّقِ has been dropped.
- إِيَّاكَ وَالْأَسَدَ is used instead of اِتَّقِ نَفْسَكَ مِنَ الْأَسَدِ to give the same meaning, which is "Save yourself from the lion."

---

[44] This is another term for شِبْهُ الْمُضَافِ. As mentioned earlier, it is similar to *mudaaf* in meaning.

80

Section 3.8.2[45]

مَفْعُوْلٌ مُطْلَقٌ

<u>Definition:</u> It is the مَصْدَرٌ of the فِعْلٌ that governs it and is used for the following:

- تَأْكِيدٌ (emphasis)   e.g.   ضَرَبْتُهُ ضَرْبًا   I beat him severely.
- بَيَانُ النَّوْعِ (description of type)   e.g.   جَلَسْتُ جِلْسَةَ الْقَارِئِ   I sat like a *Qari* would sit.
- بَيَانُ الْعَدَدِ (number of times)   e.g.   ضَرَبْتُهُ ضَرَبَتَيْنِ   I hit him twice.

<u>Note:</u> Sometimes, the فِعْلٌ governing مَفْعُوْلٌ مُطْلَقٌ is dropped because of context. For example, خَيْرَ مَقْدَمٍ. Originally, it was قَدِمْتَ قُدُوْمًا خَيْرَ مَقْدَمٍ, which means "You came a good coming." Here, the *fi'l* قَدِمْتَ, and قُدُوْمًا, which is the مَفْعُوْلٌ مُطْلَقٌ, have been dropped because of context. Only the صِفَةٌ of the مَفْعُوْلٌ مُطْلَقٍ, which is خَيْرَ مَقْدَمٍ, remains.

Section 3.8.3[46]

مَفْعُوْلٌ لِأَجْلِهِ / مَفْعُوْلٌ لَهُ

<u>Definition:</u> It is an اِسْمٌ which explains the reason for the action taking place. Generally, it is a مَصْدَرٌ.

    e.g.   ضَرَبْتُهُ تَأْدِيْبًا   I beat/hit him to teach (him) manners.

Section 3.8.4[47]

مَفْعُوْلٌ مَعَهُ

<u>Definition:</u> It is an اِسْمٌ which appears after such a وَاوٌ which has the meaning of مَعَ (with). This وَاوٌ is known as وَاوُ الْمَعِيَّةِ.

    e.g.   جَاءَ زَيْدٌ وَالْكِتَابَ   Zayd came <u>with</u> the book.

                جِئْتُ وَزَيْدًا   I came <u>with</u> Zayd.

---

[45] For more details, examples, and exercises, please refer to *al-Nahw al-Wadih*, *Ibtida'iyyah*, vol. 2, 156-160. For additional types of مَفْعُوْلٌ مُطْلَقٌ, with accompanying examples and exercises, please refer to *al-Nahw al-Wadih*, *Thanawiyyah*, vol. 1, 127-130.

[46] For more details, examples, and exercises, please refer to *al-Nahw al-Wadih*, *Ibtida'iyyah*, vol. 2, 161-164.

[47] For more details, examples and exercises, please refer to *al-Nahw al-Wadih*, *Ibtida'iyyah*, vol. 3, 157-162.

Section 3.8.5

ظَرْفٌ / مَفْعُولٌ فِيهِ

Definition: It is an اِسْمٌ which denotes the time (زَمَانٌ) or place (مَكَانٌ) in which an action took place.

e.g.   سَافَرْتُ شَهْرًا   I travelled for a month.

Both types of ظُرُوفٌ namely, زَمَانٌ and مَكَانٌ, are of two types: مَحْدُودٌ (limited, restricted) and مُبْهَمٌ (unlimited, unrestricted).

- <u>Types of ظُرُوفُ الزَّمَانِ</u>

   i.   مَحْدُودٌ (limited, restricted): for example,

يَوْمٌ	day	e.g.	صُمْتُ يَوْمًا	I fasted for one day.
لَيْلٌ	night	e.g.	عَمِلْتُ لَيْلًا	I worked for one night.
شَهْرٌ	month	e.g.	صُمْتُ شَهْرًا	I fasted for a month.
سَنَةٌ	year	e.g.	سَافَرْتُ سَنَةً	I travelled for a year.

   ii.   مُبْهَمٌ (unlimited, unrestricted): for example,

   دَهْرٌ   long period of time

      e.g.   صُمْتُ دَهْرًا   I fasted for a long time.

   حِينٌ   some time (could be short or long period of time)

      e.g.   دَعَا نُوحٌ قَوْمَهُ حِينًا مِنَ الدَّهْرِ

      Nuh (peace be upon him) called his people for some time.

- <u>Types of ظُرُوفُ الْمَكَانِ</u>

   i.   مَحْدُودٌ (limited, restricted):

      e.g.   صَلَّيْتُ فِي الْمَسْجِدِ   I prayed in the mosque.

      e.g.   جَلَسْتُ فِي الدَّارِ   I sat in the house.

   ii.   مُبْهَمٌ (unlimited, unrestricted):

خَلْفَ	behind	e.g.	جَلَسْتُ خَلْفَهُ	I sat behind him.
أَمَامَ	in front of	e.g.	قُمْتُ أَمَامَهُ	I stood in front of him.

Note: In the case of مَكَانٌ (مَحْدُودٌ), the preposition فِي is mentioned in words; while in the case of مَكَانٌ (مُبْهَمٌ), it is assumed to exist (مُقَدَّرٌ).

82

The above-mentioned five *maf'ools* have been combined in a couplet, which is as follows:

حَمِدْتُ حَمْدًا حَامِدًا وَحَمِيْدًا

رِعَايَةَ شُكْرِهِ دَهْرًا مَّدِيْدًا

I praised Haamid a lot, with Hameed,
out of regard for thanking him, for an extended period of time.

Sentence Analysis:

1. مُضَافٌ + مُضَافٌ إِلَيْهِ = شُكْرِهِ

مُضَافٌ + مُضَافٌ إِلَيْهِ = رِعَايَةَ شُكْرِهِ

2. صِفَةٌ = مَّدِيْدًا

مَوْصُوْفٌ = دَهْرًا

دَهْرًا مَّدِيْدًا	رِعَايَةَ شُكْرِهِ	وَحَمِيْدًا	حَامِدًا	حَمْدًا	حَمِدْتُ
مَفْعُوْلٌ فِيْهِ = جُمْلَةٌ فِعْلِيَّةٌ خَبَرِيَّةٌ	مَفْعُوْلٌ لَهُ	مَفْعُوْلٌ مَعَهُ	مَفْعُوْلٌ بِهِ	مَفْعُوْلٌ مُطْلَقٌ	(فِعْلٌ + فَاعِلٌ)

EXERCISE

1. Translate, fill in the *i'raab* and identify the type of مَفْعُوْلٌ in the following sentences.

viii. سافر زيد طلبا للرزق		i. أكل عليّ أكلتين	
ix. وقف الشرطي وقوف النشاط		ii. ركب إبراهيم الحصان	
x. قرأت الدرس صباحا أمام المعلم		iii. سافرت وأخاك	
xi. تدور الأرض دورة في اليوم		iv. يثب النمر وثوب الأسد	
xii. اعملوا الخير حبا في الخير		v. يسافر خالد إلى مصر طلبا للعلم	
xiii. جلست الهرة تحت المكتب		vi. لا تبخلوا خشية الفقر	
xiv. سارت السيارة ساعة		vii. توقد المصابيح ليلا	

Section 3.8.6[48]

حَالٌ – State / Condition

Definition: It is an اِسْمٌ which describes the condition of either the فَاعِلٌ or the مَفْعُوْلٌ or both at the time the action contained in the فِعْلٌ takes place.

e.g.	جَاءَ زَيْدٌ رَاكِبًا	Zayd came while mounted/riding.
	جِئْتُ زَيْدًا نَائِمًا	I came to Zayd while he was sleeping.
	كَلَّمْتُ زَيْدًا جَالِسَيْنِ	I spoke to Zayd while both of us were sitting.

Notes:

1. The condition itself is known as حَالٌ, whereas the one whose condition is being described is known as ذُو الْحَالِ.

2. The حَالٌ gets a نَصْبٌ, which is generally in the form of two *fathahs*.

3. The ذُو الْحَالِ is generally مَعْرِفَةٌ and the حَالٌ is generally نَكِرَةٌ.

   e.g.   جَاءَ زَيْدٌ رَاكِبًا   Zayd came riding/while he was mounted.

4. If the ذُو الْحَالِ is نَكِرَةٌ, the حَالٌ is brought before the ذُو الْحَالِ.

   e.g.   جَاءَنِيْ رَاكِبًا رَجُلٌ   A man came to me riding/while he was mounted.

5. The ذُو الْحَالِ can be a ضَمِيْرٌ.

   e.g.   زَيْدٌ أَكَلَ جَالِسًا   Zayd ate sitting.

   Here, the ذُو الْحَالِ is هُوَ, which is the hidden ضَمِيْرٌ in أَكَلَ.

6. The حَالٌ can be a sentence.

   - If the حَالٌ is a جُمْلَةٌ اِسْمِيَّةٌ, then a وَاوٌ (with or without a ضَمِيْرٌ) is added to give the meaning of حَالٌ.

     e.g.   لَا تَقْرَبُوا الصَّلٰوةَ وَأَنْتُمْ سُكْرٰى   Don't come near *salah* while you are intoxicated.

   - If the حَالٌ is a جُمْلَةٌ فِعْلِيَّةٌ and the فِعْلٌ is اَلْفِعْلُ الْمَاضِيْ, قَدْ has to appear before the اَلْفِعْلُ الْمَاضِيْ.

     e.g.   جَاءَ زَيْدٌ وَقَدْ خَرَجَ خَادِمُهُ   Zayd came while his servant had left.

---

[48] For more details, examples and exercises, please refer to *al-Nahw al-Wadih, Ibtida'iyyah*, vol. 3, 101-109.

Sentence Analysis:

1. جَاءَ زَيْدٌ رَاكِبًا   Zayd came riding/while he was mounted.

$$\underset{|}{\text{جَاءَ}} \qquad \underset{\text{حَالٌ}}{\overline{\text{زَيْدٌ}}} + \underset{\text{ذُو الْحَالِ}}{\overline{\text{رَاكِبًا}}}$$

جُمْلَةٌ فِعْلِيَّةٌ خَبَرِيَّةٌ = فَاعِلٌ + فِعْلٌ

2. جِئْتُ عَمْرًا نَائِمًا   I came to 'Amr while he was asleep.

$$\underset{|}{\text{جِئْتُ}} \qquad \underset{\text{حَالٌ}}{\overline{\text{عَمْرًا}}} + \underset{\text{ذُو الْحَالِ}}{\overline{\text{نَائِمًا}}}$$

جُمْلَةٌ فِعْلِيَّةٌ خَبَرِيَّةٌ = مَفْعُولٌ بِهِ + فِعْلٌ + فَاعِلٌ

3. لَقِيتُ بَكْرًا وَهُوَ جَالِسٌ I met Bakr while he was sitting.

$$\underset{|}{\text{لَقِيتُ}} \qquad \underset{|}{\text{بَكْرًا}} \qquad \underset{|}{\text{وَ}} \qquad \underset{\text{مُبْتَدَأٌ}}{\text{هُوَ}} \quad \underset{\text{خَبَرٌ}}{\text{جَالِسٌ}} = \text{جُمْلَةٌ اسْمِيَّةٌ خَبَرِيَّةٌ}$$

ذُو الْحَالِ + وَاوٌ حَالِيَّةٌ + حَالٌ

(فِعْلٌ + فَاعِلٌ) + مَفْعُولٌ بِهِ = جُمْلَةٌ فِعْلِيَّةٌ خَبَرِيَّةٌ

4. زَيْدٌ أَكَلَ جَالِسًا   Zayd ate while sitting.

$$\underset{}{\text{زَيْدٌ}} \qquad \underset{\text{فِيهِ ضَمِيرٌ مُسْتَتَرٌ (هُوَ)}}{\text{أَكَلَ}} \qquad \underset{|}{\text{جَالِسًا}}$$

حَالٌ + ذُو الْحَالِ

فِعْلٌ (أَكَلَ) + فَاعِلٌ = جُمْلَةٌ فِعْلِيَّةٌ خَبَرِيَّةٌ

مُبْتَدَأٌ + خَبَرٌ = جُمْلَةٌ اسْمِيَّةٌ خَبَرِيَّةٌ

85

EXERCISE

1. Translate, fill in the *i'raab* and point out the حَالٌ and ذُو الْحَالِ in the following sentences.

i.	أحب التلميذ مجتهدا	vi.	لا تأكلوا الطعام حارا
ii.	لقيت زيدا راكبين	vii.	نصرت زيدا مشدودا
iii.	لا تأكلوا الفاكهة وهي فجة	viii.	غاب أخوك وقد حضر جميع أصدقاءه
iv.	رجع القائد منصورا	ix.	دخل اللص المنزل وأهله نائمون
v.	قطف التاجر العنب ناضجا	x.	نمت الأشجار ولما يثمر

86

<u>Section 3.8.7</u>[49]

تَمْيِيزٌ / تَمَيُّزٌ

<u>Definition:</u> It is an اِسْمٌ نَكِرَةٌ which removes the ambiguity or vagueness created by the preceding اِسْمٌ. This ambiguity may be in distance, weight, measure, number, etc.

   e.g.   رَأَيْتُ أَحَدَ عَشَرَ كَوْكَبًا   I saw eleven stars.

   Here, the word (كَوْكَبًا) clarifies what (أَحَدَ عَشَرَ) refers to.

<u>Sentence Analysis:</u>

رَأَيْتُ	أَحَدَ عَشَرَ	كَوْكَبًا
	مُمَيَّزٌ	+	تَمْيِيزٌ

فِعْلٌ + فَاعِلٌ   +   مَفْعُوْلٌ بِهِ   =   جُمْلَةٌ فِعْلِيَّةٌ خَبَرِيَّةٌ

<u>Notes:</u>

- The ambiguous اِسْمٌ is called مُمَيَّزٌ and the اِسْمٌ which clarifies it is called تَمْيِيزٌ or تَمَيُّزٌ.
- The تَمْيِيزٌ is *mansoob* and gets two *fathahs*.
- Sometimes, the مُمَيَّزٌ is not mentioned in words but is understood from the meaning of the sentence (مَلْحُوْظٌ).

   e.g.   حَسُنَ الْوَلَدُ كَلَامًا   The boy is good in terms of (his) speech.

- If the مُمَيَّزٌ is a number, the rules with regards to the usage of numerals (on the next page) must be kept in mind.

EXERCISE

1. Translate, fill in the *i'raab* and point out the مُمَيَّزٌ and تَمْيِيزٌ in the following sentences.

i.	فى الحقل عشرون بقرة	v.	طاب المكان هواء
ii.	بعته ذراعا حريرا	vi.	لا أملك شبرا أرضا
iii.	الفيل أكبر من الجمل جسما	vii.	شربت رطلا لبنا
iv.	أطعمت الدجاجة ملء الكف حبا	viii.	شربت كوبا ماء

---

[49] For more details, examples and exercises, please refer to *al-Nahw al-Wadih, Ibtida'iyyah*, vol. 3, 110-119.

Rules for أَسْمَاءُ الْعَدَدِ (numerals)

Before we proceed, it should be pointed out that

عَدَدٌ (number) is the مُمَيَّز   and   مَعْدُودٌ (the counted *ism*) is the تَمْيِيزٌ.

One and two (1-2)

- The مَعْدُودٌ appears first and the عَدَدٌ appears second.
- The عَدَدٌ and the مَعْدُودٌ must correspond in all aspects.

  e.g.   وَلَدٌ وَاحِدٌ   one boy

           بِنْتٌ وَاحِدَةٌ   one girl

  <u>Note:</u> Normally, for one or two boys, girls, men etc., one simply says وَلَدٌ or وَلَدَانِ, etc. However, at times, the number is used for emphasis.

Three through ten (3-10)

- From three onwards, the عَدَدٌ appears first and the مَعْدُودٌ second.
- The مَعْدُودٌ is جَمْعٌ مَجْرُورٌ.
- The عَدَدٌ and the مَعْدُودٌ must be of opposite gender.

  e.g.   ثَلَاثَةُ أَقْلَامٍ   three pens

           خَمْسُ سَيَّارَاتٍ   five cars

  <u>Note:</u> In choosing the correct عَدَدٌ gender, the singular form of the مَعْدُودٌ is taken into account.

       e.g.   سَبْعَ لَيَالٍ وَثَمَانِيَةَ أَيَّامٍ   seven nights and eight days

  Here, the singular لَيْلَةٌ (night) of لَيَالٍ is feminine, and يَوْمٌ (day) of أَيَّامٍ is masculine.

- For ten, the masculine form is عَشْرٌ, and the feminine form is عَشَرَةٌ.

Eleven and twelve (11-12)

- From eleven onwards till 99, the مَعْدُودٌ is وَاحِدٌ مَنْصُوبٌ.
- The عَدَدٌ and the مَعْدُودٌ must have the same gender.

  e.g.   أَحَدَ عَشَرَ كَوْكَبًا   eleven stars

           اِثْنَتَا عَشْرَةَ بِنْتًا   twelve girls

- From 11–19, the ش of عشرة/عشر gets a *fathah* when used with a masculine and a *sukoon* when used with a feminine.[50]

---

[50] For feminine, the form عَشَرَة is also used. See W. Wright, *Arabic Grammar*, (Mineola, NY: Dover Publications, 2005), Part 1, 256. Also see *Sharh ibn 'Aqil*, vol. 4, 71.

Thirteen through nineteen (13-19)

- The مَعْدُوْدٌ is وَاحِدٌ مَنْصُوْبٌ.
- The gender of the first part of the عَدَدٌ should be opposite of the gender of the مَعْدُوْدٌ.

  e.g. أَرْبَعَةَ عَشَرَ رَجُلًا   fourteen men

  تِسْعَ عَشْرَةَ بِنْتًا   nineteen girls

- The "ten" عشر (masc.)/عشرة (fem.) agrees with the مَعْدُوْدٌ in terms of gender.

Twenty till ninety (20, 30, 40,...,90)

- The مَعْدُوْدٌ is وَاحِدٌ مَنْصُوْبٌ.
- The gender of عِشْرُوْنَ to تِسْعُوْنَ (20,30,40,...90) remains the same irrespective of whether the مَعْدُوْدٌ is masculine or feminine.

  e.g. عِشْرُوْنَ رَجُلًا   twenty men

  ثَلَاثُوْنَ بِنْتًا   thirty girls

Twenty-one and twenty-two (21-22)

- The مَعْدُوْدٌ is وَاحِدٌ مَنْصُوْبٌ.
- The first part of the عَدَدٌ and the مَعْدُوْدٌ must have the same gender.

  e.g. وَاحِدٌ وَعِشْرُوْنَ رَجُلًا   twenty-one men

  إِحْدَى وَعِشْرُوْنَ بِنْتًا   twenty-one girls

- The same will apply to 31-32, 41-42...91-92.

Twenty-three through twenty-nine (23-29)

- The مَعْدُوْدٌ is وَاحِدٌ مَنْصُوْبٌ.
- The gender of the first part of the عَدَدٌ should be opposite of the gender of the مَعْدُوْدٌ.

  e.g. أَرْبَعَةٌ وَعِشْرُوْنَ رَجُلًا   twenty-four men

  سِتٌّ وَعِشْرُوْنَ بِنْتًا   twenty-six girls

- The same applies to 33-39, 43-49...93-99.
- The "tens" remain the same, irrespective of whether the مَعْدُوْدٌ is masculine or feminine.

Hundred (100)

- The مَعْدُوْد is وَاحِدٌ مَجْرُوْرٌ.
- مِائَة remains the same irrespective of whether the مَعْدُوْد is masculine or feminine.

  e.g.   مِائَةُ رَجُلٍ   hundred men   مِائَةُ بِنْتٍ   hundred girls

- For 200, مِائَتَا is used. (حَالَةُ النَّصْبِ وَ الْجَرِّ in مِائَتَيْ)

  e.g.   مِائَتَا بِنْتٍ   two hundred girls

  مِائَتَيْ بِنْتٍtwo hundred girls

- Since مِائَةٌ is feminine, the number **before** مِائَة is masculine.

  e.g.   أَرْبَعُمِائَةِ رَجُلٍ   four hundred men

  أَرْبَعُمِائَةِ بِنْتٍ   four hundred women

- If there are units and tens with the 100's as well, their respective gender rules apply.

  e.g.   مِائَةٌ وَعَشَرَةُ كُتُبٍ   hundred and ten books

  مِائَةٌ وَخَمْسٌ وَأَرْبَعُوْنَ كُرَّاسَةً   hundred and forty-five note-books

Thousand (1,000)

- The مَعْدُوْد is وَاحِدٌ مَجْرُوْرٌ.
- أَلْف remains the same, irrespective of whether the مَعْدُوْد is masculine or feminine.

  e.g.   أَلْفُ رَجُلٍ   thousand men   أَلْفُ بِنْتٍ   thousand girls

- Since أَلْفٌ is masculine, the number **before** أَلْف is feminine.

  e.g.   أَرْبَعَةُ آلَافِ رَجُلٍ   four thousand men

  أَرْبَعَةُ آلَافِ بِنْتٍ   four thousand women

  <u>Note</u>: The plural for أَلْفٌ is آلَافٍ.

Million (1,000,000)

- The مَعْدُوْد is وَاحِدٌ مَجْرُوْرٌ.
- مِلْيُوْن remains the same irrespective of whether the مَعْدُوْد is masculine or feminine.

  e.g.   مِلْيُوْنُ رَجُلٍ   million men

  مِلْيُوْنُ بِنْتٍ   million girls

- Since مِلْيُوْنٌ is masculine, the number **before** مِلْيُوْنٌ is feminine.

  e.g.   أَرْبَعَةُ مَلَايِيْنَ رَجُلٍ   four million men

  أَرْبَعَةُ مَلَايِيْنَ اِمْرَأَةٍ   four million women

  <u>Note</u>: The plural for مِلْيُوْنٌ is مَلَايِيْنٌ.

EXERCISES

1. Write the following in Arabic.

   i. 2 schools

   ii. 12 women

   iii. 17 doors

   iv. 21 cars

   v. 150 houses

   vi. 444 miles

   vii. 11 books

   viii. 14 chairs

   ix. 26 boys

   x. 111 elephants

   xi. 195 keys

   xii. 3,333 roses

2. Translate the following sentences and fill in the *i'raab*.

   i. في البستان تسع وتسعون نخلة

   ii. مساحة الدار ألفا ذراع

   iii. للحجرة ثلاثة شبابيك

   iv. باع التاجر أربعة عشر قنطارا قطنا

   v. في الكتاب أربع وعشرون صفحة

   vi. في السنة اثنا عشر شهرا

   vii. عمر أخيك الآن خمس وثلاثون سنة

   viii. باضت الدجاجة ثلاث بيضات

مُسْتَثْنَى

اِسْتِثْنَاءٌ   means to exclude.

مُسْتَثْنَى   is an اِسْمٌ which has been excluded and appears after the حَرْفُ الْاِسْتِثْنَاءِ.

مُسْتَثْنَى مِنْهُ is an اِسْمٌ from which the مُسْتَثْنَى has been excluded. It appears before حَرْفُ الْاِسْتِثْنَاءِ.

حُرُوفُ الْاِسْتِثْنَاءِ are as follows:

مَا عَدَا   مَا خَلَا   عَدَا   خَلَا   حَاشَا   سِوَى   غَيْرَ   إِلَّا

e.g.   جَاءَ الْقَوْمُ إِلَّا زَيْدًا   The people came except Zayd.

زَيْدًا	إِلَّا	الْقَوْمُ	جَاءَ
مُسْتَثْنَى +	حَرْفُ الْاِسْتِثْنَاءِ +	مُسْتَثْنَى مِنْهُ	

جُمْلَةٌ فِعْلِيَّةٌ خَبَرِيَّةٌ   =   فَاعِلٌ   +   فِعْلٌ

Related terminology

مُسْتَثْنَى مُتَّصِلٌ   refers to the case when the مُسْتَثْنَى was included in the مُسْتَثْنَى مِنْهُ before the اِسْتِثْنَاءٌ.

e.g.   جَاءَ الْقَوْمُ إِلَّا زَيْدًا   The people came except Zayd.

(Zayd was one of the people before the exclusion.)

مُسْتَثْنَى مُنْقَطِعٌ   refers to the case when the مُسْتَثْنَى was not included in the مُسْتَثْنَى مِنْهُ before the اِسْتِثْنَاءٌ.

e.g.   سَجَدَ الْمَلَائِكَةُ إِلَّا إِبْلِيسَ   The angels prostrated except Iblees.

(Iblees was never one of the angels.)

جَاءَ الْقَوْمُ إِلَّا حِمَارًا   The people came except a donkey.

(Donkey was never included among the people.)

كَلَامٌ مُثْبَتٌ/كَلَامٌ مُوْجَبٌ (positive statement) refers to a sentence which does not have a نَفْيٌ, نَهْيٌ or اِسْتِفْهَامٌ.

e.g.   جَاءَ الْقَوْمُ إِلَّا زَيْدًا   The people came except Zayd.

كَلَامٌ مَنْفِيٌّ/كَلَامٌ غَيْرُ مُوْجَبٍ (negative sentence) refers to a sentence which does have a نَفْيٌ, نَهْيٌ or اِسْتِفْهَامٌ.

e.g.   مَا جَاءَ الْقَوْمُ إِلَّا زَيْدًا   The people did not come except Zayd.

---

[51] For more details, examples and exercises, please refer to *al-Nahw al-Wadih*, *Ibtida'iyyah*, vol. 3, 88-100.

مُسْتَثْنًى مُفَرَّغٌ refers to a sentence in which the مُسْتَثْنًى مِنْهُ is not mentioned.

e.g.   مَا جَاءَ إِلَّا زَيْدٌ   No one came except Zayd.

مُسْتَثْنًى غَيْرُ مُفَرَّغٍ refers to a sentence in which the مُسْتَثْنًى مِنْهُ is mentioned.

e.g.   جَاءَ الْقَوْمُ إِلَّا زَيْدًا   The people came except Zayd.

The *i'raab* of the various types of مُسْتَثْنًى are given below:

Table 3.8

إِعْرَابُ الْمُسْتَثْنَى

حُرُوفُ الِاسْتِثْنَاءِ	Sentence Type			إِعْرَابُ الْمُسْتَثْنَى	Example
1. إِلَّا	مُنْقَطِعٌ			مَنْصُوبٌ	سَجَدَ الْمَلَائِكَةُ إِلَّا إِبْلِيسَ The angels prostrated except Iblees.
2. إِلَّا	مُتَّصِلٌ	مُوجَبٌ		مَنْصُوبٌ	جَاءَنِي الْقَوْمُ إِلَّا زَيْدًا The people came to me except zayd.
3. إِلَّا	مُتَّصِلٌ	غَيْرُ مُوجَبٍ	غَيْرُ مُفَرَّغٍ	مَنْصُوبٌ – or – same as مُسْتَثْنَى مِنْهُ	مَا جَاءَنِي أَحَدٌ إِلَّا زَيْدًا مَا جَاءَنِي أَحَدٌ إِلَّا زَيْدٌ No one came to me except Zayd.
4. إِلَّا	مُتَّصِلٌ	غَيْرُ مُوجَبٍ	مُفَرَّغٌ	according to the عَامِلٌ governing مُسْتَثْنَى مِنْهُ (as if إِلَّا does not exist)	مَا جَاءَ إِلَّا زَيْدٌ No one came except Zayd. مَا رَأَيْتُ إِلَّا زَيْدًا I did not see anyone except Zayd. مَا مَرَرْتُ إِلَّا بِزَيْدٍ I did not pass by anyone except Zayd.
5. مَا خَلَا – مَا عَدَا	All types			مَنْصُوبٌ	جَاءَ الْقَوْمُ مَا خَلَا زَيْدًا جَاءَ الْقَوْمُ مَا عَدَا زَيْدًا The people came except Zayd.

93

Table 3.8 – *Continued*

حُرُوْفُ الْاِسْتِثْنَاءِ	Sentence Type	إِعْرَابُ الْمُسْتَثْنَى	Example
6. خَلَا – عَدَا – حَاشَا	All types	– or – مَنْصُوْبٌ مَجْرُوْرٌ (as a preposition)	جَاءَ الْقَوْمُ خَلَا/عَدَا/حَاشَا زَيْدًا جَاءَ الْقَوْمُ خَلَا/عَدَا/حَاشَا زَيْدٍ The people came except Zayd.
7. غَيْرُ – سِوَى	All types	مَجْرُوْرٌ	جَاءَ الْقَوْمُ غَيْرَ زَيْدٍ جَاءَ الْقَوْمُ سِوَى زَيْدٍ The people came except Zayd.

<u>Note:</u> The *i'raab* of the word غَيْرُ is the same as that of مُسْتَثْنَى بِ إِلَّا. Thus, the simple way to determine the *i'raab* of غَيْرُ is to replace غَيْرُ with إِلَّا. Now, whatever *i'raab* مُسْتَثْنَى was supposed to get, should be given to غَيْرُ.

For example, we have two sentences, 1) جَاءَ الْقَوْمُ غَيْرَ زَيْدٍ and 2) مَا جَاءَ غَيْرُ زَيْدٍ.

To determine the *i'raab* of غَيْرُ, follow the following two steps for each of these sentences.

a. Replace غير with إِلَّا and see what the *i'raab* of the مُسْتَثْنَى would be.

2) مَا جَاءَ إِلَّا زَيْدٌ   1) جَاءَ الْقَوْمُ إِلَّا زَيْدًا

The first sentence is مُوْجَبٌ, so the مُسْتَثْنَى will be *mansoob*. The second sentence is غَيْرُ مُوْجَبٍ and مُفَرَّغٌ, so the مُسْتَثْنَى is according to the *'aamil*. Thus, it will be *marfoo'*.

b. The *i'raab* of the مُسْتَثْنَى (with إِلَّا) will be given to غَيْرُ.

2) مَا جَاءَ غَيْرُ زَيْدٍ   1) جَاءَ الْقَوْمُ غَيْرَ زَيْدٍ

<u>EXERCISES</u>

1. Translate, fill in the *i'raab* and explain the *i'raab* of the *mustathnaa*.

    i. رأيت الجنود إلا القائد   v. دخلت غرف البيت خلا غرفة النوم

    ii. صام الغلام رمضان غير يوم   vi. ما عاد المريض عائد غير الطبيب

    iii. زرت مساجد المدينة ما خلا واحدا   vii. قرأت الكتاب إلا صفحتين

    iv. جاء القوم إلا حمارا   viii. ما جاء إلا معلم

Section 3.9[52]
اَلْمَجْرُوْرَاتُ – Words which are always *majroor*

There are two types of words that are always *majroor*. These are as follows:

1. An اِسْمٌ preceded by a حَرْفُ جَرٍّ.

    e.g.   فِي الْكِتَابِ   in the book

2. مُضَافٌ إِلَيْهِ

    e.g.   كِتَابُ زَيْدٍ   book of Zayd

---

[52] For more examples and exercises, please refer to *al-Nahw al-Wadih*, *Ibtida'iyyah*, vol. 1, 76-81.

Section 3.10

اَلتَّوَابِعُ

Definition: A تَابِعٌ is an اِسْمٌ which follows the اِسْمٌ before it in terms of i'raab (and some other things which vary from تَابِعٌ to تَابِعٌ). The preceding اِسْمٌ is called the مَتْبُوعٌ.

- The عَامِلٌ which governs the مَتْبُوعٌ also governs the تَابِعٌ.
- There are five تَوَابِعُ:

(3) اَلْبَدَلُ	(2) اَلتَّأْكِيدُ/اَلتَّوْكِيدُ	(1) اَلنَّعْتُ/اَلصِّفَةُ
	(5) اَلْعَطْفُ بِحَرْفٍ/عَطْفُ النَّسَقِ	(4) عَطْفُ الْبَيَانِ

Section 3.10.1[53]
اَلنَّعْتُ أَوْ اَلصِّفَةُ – Adjective[54]

اَلنَّعْتُ/اَلصِّفَةُ is of two types: 1) نَعْتٌ حَقِيقِيٌّ   2) نَعْتٌ سَبَبِيٌّ

1. <u>نَعْتٌ حَقِيقِيٌّ</u>: It is a word which describes the actual مَتْبُوعٌ.
   - As mentioned in section 1.4.3, the نَعْتٌ follows the مَنْعُوتٌ, which is the مَتْبُوعٌ in this case, in the following:

     a. I'raab   b. Gender

     c. Being ma'rifah or nakirah   d. Being singular, dual or plural
   - The نَعْتٌ can be a complete sentence, in which case the مَنْعُوتٌ must be نَكِرَةٌ.
   - The نَعْتٌ which is a sentence must have a ضَمِيرٌ which refers to the نَكِرَةٌ مَنْعُوتٌ.

     e.g.   جَاءَنِيْ وَلَدٌ يَرْكَبُ الدَّرَّاجَةَ   A boy who was riding the bicycle came to me.

الدَّرَّاجَةَ	يَرْكَبُ	وَلَدٌ	نِيْ	جَاءَ
فِعْلٌ + فَاعِلٌ (هُوَ) + مَفْعُوْلٌ بِهِ				

نَعْتٌ   +   نَكِرَةٌ مَنْعُوْتٌ

فِعْلٌ + مَفْعُوْلٌ + فَاعِلٌ

= جُمْلَةٌ فِعْلِيَّةٌ خَبَرِيَّةٌ

---

[53] For more details, examples and exercises, please refer to *al-Nahw al-Wadih, Ibtida'iyyah*, vol. 3, 134-142.

[54] نَعْتٌ is another name for صِفَةٌ; and مَنْعُوْتٌ is another name for مَوْصُوْفٌ.

96

Note:

- If a مَعْرِفَة is followed by a sentence, it will be a خَبَرٌ or حَالٌ.

  Example 1   اَلْوَلَدُ يَرْكَبُ الدَّرَّاجَةَ   The boy is riding the bicycle.

  Here, (اَلْوَلَدُ) is مُبْتَدَأٌ, and (يَرْكَبُ الدَّرَّاجَةَ) is the خَبَرٌ.

  Example 2   جَاءَنِي الْوَلَدُ يَرْكَبُ الدَّرَّاجَةَ

  The boy came to me while riding the bicycle.

  Here, (اَلْوَلَدُ) is ذُو الْحَالِ, and (يَرْكَبُ الدَّرَّاجَةَ) is the حَالٌ.

Sentence Analysis

1. جَاءَ رَجُلٌ عَالِمٌ   A learned man came.

عَالِمٌ	رَجُلٌ	جَاءَ
نَعْتٌ (تَابِعٌ) +	مَنْعُوْتٌ (مَتْبُوْعٌ)		

جُمْلَةٌ فِعْلِيَّةٌ خَبَرِيَّةٌ =   فَاعِلٌ   +   فِعْلٌ

2. جَاءَ رَجُلٌ أَبُوْهُ عَالِمٌ   A man whose father is learned, came.

عَالِمٌ	أَبُوْهُ	رَجُلٌ	جَاءَ
	(مُضَافٌ وَمُضَافٌ إِلَيْهِ)		

جُمْلَةٌ اِسْمِيَّةٌ خَبَرِيَّةٌ (نَكِرَةٌ) = خَبَرٌ + مُبْتَدَأٌ

نَعْتٌ (تَابِعٌ) + مَنْعُوْتٌ (مَتْبُوْعٌ)

جُمْلَةٌ فِعْلِيَّةٌ خَبَرِيَّةٌ =   فَاعِلٌ   +   فِعْلٌ

2. نَعْتٌ سَبَبِيٌّ: It is a word which does not describe the مَتْبُوْعٌ, but describes that which is connected to the مَتْبُوْعٌ.

  e.g.   جَاءَنِيْ وَلَدٌ عَالِمٌ أَبُوْهُ   A boy whose father is learned, came to me.

  Here, عَالِمٌ is describing أَبُوْهُ, which is connected to the مَتْبُوْعٌ (وَلَدٌ). In other words, it is describing the مَتْبُوْعٌ indirectly.

Notes:

1. In نَعْتٌ سَبَبِيٌّ, the مَنْعُوْتٌ and نَعْتٌ must correspond in only two aspects:
   a. *I'raab*
   b. Being *ma'rifah* or *nakirah*

2. The نَعْتٌ will always be singular, irrespective of whether the مَنْعُوْتٌ is singular, dual or plural.

    e.g.   هَاتَانِ صُوْرَتَانِ جَمِيْلٌ إِطَارَاهُمَا   These are two pictures whose frames are beautiful.

3. The نَعْتٌ will correspond in gender to the word **after it**.

    e.g.   جَاءَتِ السَّيِّدَةُ الْعَاقِلُ وَلَدُهَا   The lady, whose son is intelligent, came.

Sentence Analysis:

1.   جَاءَتْ امْرَأَةٌ عَالِمٌ ابْنُهَا   A woman whose son is learned, came.

ابْنُهَا	عَالِمٌ	امْرَأَةٌ	جَاءَتْ
(مُضَافٌ وَمُضَافٌ إِلَيْهِ)			
جُمْلَةٌ فِعْلِيَّةٌ خَبَرِيَّة =	فَاعِلُ "عَالِمٌ" + اسْمُ الْفَاعِلِ		
	نَعْتٌ (تَابِعٌ) + مَنْعُوْتٌ (مَتْبُوْعٌ)		
جُمْلَةٌ فِعْلِيَّةٌ خَبَرِيَّة =	فَاعِلٌ	+	فِعْلٌ

Note: In this example, عَالِمٌ is the نَعْتٌ سَبَبِيٌّ of امْرَأَةٌ. Because of امْرَأَةٌ, it is *marfoo'* and نَكِرَةٌ. However, it follows ابْنُهَا, or more precisely ابْنٌ, in being masculine.[55]

EXERCISE

1. Translate, fill in the i'raab and point out the نَعْتٌ حَقِيْقِيٌّ and the نَعْتٌ سَبَبِيٌّ in the following sentences.

    i.   ركبت الحصان الجميل سرجه   v.   أوقدت مصباحا نوره قوي

    ii.   هو رجل عالمة ابنته   vi.   هذا عمل ينفع

    iii. هؤلاء بنات عاقلات   vii. هذا منزل ضيق

    iv.   شاهدنا قطارا سيره سريع   viii. جاء الرجل المهذب أخوه

---

[55] There seems to be a contradiction between the sentence analysis and the note given above for نَعْتٌ سَبَبِيٌّ. All the books of *Nahw* that I referred to, including *'Ilm al-Nahw*, *al-Nahw al-Wadih*, and *Sharh ibn 'Aqil*, agree that in this example, only عَالِمٌ is the نَعْتٌ سَبَبِيٌّ. Yet, in *'Ilm al-Nahw*, the author, Mawlana Charthawali, after explaining the rules for نَعْتٌ سَبَبِيٌّ, has given this example of sentence analysis, in which he makes عَالِمٌ ابْنُهَا the نَعْتٌ of امْرَأَةٌ. This suggests that there can be two ways of looking at this.

2. Analyze the following sentences and and point out the difference between them.

       i.   هذا الولد ضاحك   iii.   جاء الولد ضاحكا

      ii.   هذا ولد ضاحك

<u>Section 3.10.2</u>[56]

اَلتَّوْكِيدُ / اَلتَّأْكِيدُ – Emphasis

<u>Definition:</u> It is a تَابِعٌ which emphasizes the مَتْبُوعٌ in the matter related to it or emphasizes the inclusion of all members of the مَتْبُوعٌ in the matter related to it.

e.g.	جَاءَنِي زَيْدٌ زَيْدٌ	(The second 'Zayd' emphasized Zayd's coming.)
	جَاءَ الْقَوْمُ كُلُّهُمْ	(كُلُّهُمْ emphasized that all came, no one remained.)

- The تَابِعٌ is called تَأْكِيدٌ and the مَتْبُوعٌ is called مُؤَكَّدٌ.

There are two types of تَأْكِيدٌ: لَفْظِيٌّ and مَعْنَوِيٌّ:

1. اَلتَّوْكِيدُ اللَّفْظِيُّ – Verbal emphasis: The emphasis is attained by repeating the مُؤَكَّدٌ which may be إِسْمٌ, فِعْلٌ, حَرْفٌ, ضَمِيرٌ, or sentence.

e.g.	جَاءَ زَيْدٌ زَيْدٌ	Zayd definitely came.
	حَضَرَ حَضَرَ الْغَائِبُ	The absent one definitely became present.
	لَا لَا أَخُونُ الْعَهْدَ	I will definitely not break the pledge.
	اِفْتَحْ أَنْتَ النَّافِذَةَ	*You* open the window.
	أَنْتَ الْمَلُومُ أَنْتَ الْمَلُومُ	You are, indeed, the censured one.

2. اَلتَّوْكِيدُ الْمَعْنَوِيُّ – Emphasis through meaning: The emphasis is attained with any of the following words:

أَبْتَعُ   أَبْصَعُ   أَكْتَعُ   أَجْمَعُ   كُلٌّ   كِلْتَا   كِلَا   عَيْنٌ   نَفْسٌ

Below, we discuss each of these.

a. عَيْنٌ، نَفْسٌ (himself, herself, itself)
   - These are used for singular, dual and plural.
   - They have to be مُضَافٌ to a ضَمِيرٌ.
   - Their ضَمِيرٌ must agree with the مُؤَكَّدٌ in terms of gender and singularity (or duality/plurality), while the صِيغَةٌ should agree with the مُؤَكَّدٌ in terms of singularity (or duality/plurality). The exception is that the plural صِيغَةٌ of نَفْسٌ and عَيْنٌ is used in place of the dual صِيغَةٌ.

e.g.	قَامَ زَيْدٌ نَفْسُهُ/عَيْنُهُ	Zayd himself stood.
	قَامَ الزَّيْدَانِ أَنْفُسُهُمَا/أَعْيُنُهُمَا	The two Zayds themselves stood.
	قَامَ الزَّيْدُونَ أَنْفُسُهُمْ/أَعْيُنُهُمْ	The (many) Zayds themselves stood.

---

[56] For more details, examples and exercises, please refer to *al-Nahw al-Wadih, Ibtida'iyyah*, vol. 3, 143-152

جَاءَتِ الْمُعَلِّمَةُ عَيْنُهَا/نَفْسُهَا	The female teacher herself came.
جَاءَتِ الْمُعَلِّمَتَانِ أَعْيُنُهُمَا/أَنْفُسُهُمَا	The two female teachers themselves came.
جَاءَتِ الْمُعَلِّمَاتُ أَعْيُنُهُنَّ/أَنْفُسُهُنَّ	The (many) female teachers themselves came.

b. كِلْتَا، كِلَا (both)

- These are used for dual only.
- كِلَا is masculine and كِلْتَا is feminine.
- It must be مُضَافٌ to a dual ضَمِيرٌ.

e.g.
قَامَ الرَّجُلَانِ كِلَاهُمَا	Both of the men stood up.
قَامَتِ الْمُعَلِّمَتَانِ كِلْتَاهُمَا	Both of the female teachers stood up.

c. جَمِيعٌ، أَجْمَعُ، كُلٌّ (all)

- They are used for singular and plural.
- كُلٌّ and جَمِيعٌ should be مُضَافٌ to a ضَمِيرٌ which must correspond to the مُؤَكَّد.
- أَجْمَعُ is used with its صِيغَةٌ changing to correspond to the مُؤَكَّد.

e.g.
قَرَأْتُ الْكِتَابَ كُلَّهُ	I read the whole book.
جَاءَ الرِّجَالُ كُلُّهُمْ	All the men came.
جَاءَ الرِّجَالُ جَمِيعُهُمْ	All the men came.
جَاءَ النَّاسُ أَجْمَعُونَ	All the people came.

<u>Note:</u> كُلٌّ, جَمِيعٌ and أَجْمَعُ can only be used for emphasis in those things which have parts or can be divided. Thus, أَكْرَمْتُ زَيْدًا كُلَّهُ (I treated all of Zayd hospitably) would be incorrect.

d. أَبْتَعُ، أَبْصَعُ، أَكْتَعُ

- These are used for greater emphasis.
- They appear after أَجْمَعُ. They are not used without أَجْمَعُ nor can they appear before أَجْمَعُ.

e.g.
جَاءَ الْقَوْمُ أَجْمَعُونَ أَكْتَعُونَ/أَبْتَعُونَ/أَبْصَعُونَ	All of the people came.
قَامَتِ النِّسَاءُ جُمَعُ كُتَعُ/بُتَعُ/بُصَعُ	All of the women stood up.

Sentence Analysis

جَاءَ الْقَوْمُ كُلُّهُمْ أَجْمَعُونَ   All the people came.

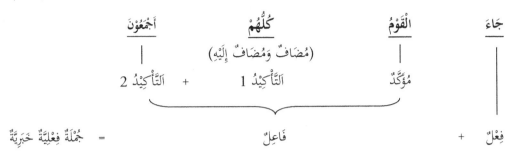

EXERCISE

1. Translate, fill in the *i'raab* and analyze the following sentences.

i. قابلت الوزير نفسه	vi. رأيت التمساح التمساح
ii. ذبحنا الكبشين كليهما	vii. قطعنا نحن أنفسنا الطريق كله
iii. سجد الملئكة كلهم أجمعون إلا ابليس	viii. الملك كله لله
iv. إياك إياك والنميمة	ix. غربت غربت الشمس
v. عاد القائد عينه	x. حذار حذار من الإهمال

102

<u>Section 3.10.3</u>[57]

<u>اَلْبَدَلُ</u> – Substitute

<u>Definition:</u> A بَدَلٌ is a تَابِعٌ which is actually intended in the sentence and not its مَتْبُوعٌ. The مَتْبُوعٌ merely serves as an introduction to the تَابِعٌ.

- The تَابِعٌ is called بَدَلٌ (substitute) and the مَتْبُوعٌ is called مُبْدَلٌ مِنْهُ or مُبَدَّلٌ مِنْهُ (the substituted).

  e.g.   جَاءَ زَيْدٌ أَخُوكَ   Zayd, your brother, came.

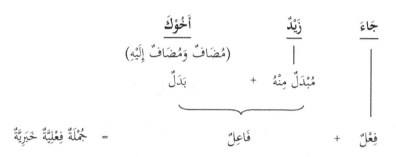

There are four types of بَدَلٌ:

1) بَدَلُ كُلٍّ مِنْ كُلٍّ   2) بَدَلُ بَعْضٍ مِنْ كُلٍّ   3) بَدَلُ الْإِشْتِمَالِ   4) بَدَلُ الْغَلَطِ

1. بَدَلُ كُلٍّ مِنْ كُلٍّ (also called بَدَلُ الْكُلِّ): It is that بَدَلٌ, which refers to the exact same thing as the مُبْدَلٌ مِنْهُ.

   e.g.   جَاءَ زَيْدٌ أَخُوكَ   Zayd, your brother, came.

2. بَدَلُ بَعْضٍ مِنْ كُلٍّ (also called بَدَلُ الْبَعْضِ): It is that بَدَلٌ, which refers to a **part** of the مُبْدَلٌ مِنْهُ.

   - The بَدَلٌ must have a ضَمِيرٌ, which refers to the مُبْدَلٌ مِنْهُ.

   e.g.   ضَرَبْتُ زَيْدًا رَأْسَهُ   I hit Zayd's head.

3. بَدَلُ الْإِشْتِمَالِ: It is that بَدَلٌ, which is related to the مُبْدَلٌ مِنْهُ, but is not part of it.

   - The بَدَلٌ must have a ضَمِيرٌ, which refers to the مُبْدَلٌ مِنْهُ.

   e.g.   سُرِقَ زَيْدٌ قَمِيْصُهُ   Zayd's shirt was stolen.

4. بَدَلُ الْغَلَطِ: It is that بَدَلٌ, which is mentioned **after an error**, as a correction.

   e.g.   إِشْتَرَيْتُ فَرَسًا حِمَارًا   I bought a horse; no, a donkey.

---

[57] For more details, examples and exercises, please refer to *al-Nahw al-Wadih, Ibtida'iyyah*, vol. 3, 163-167.

EXERCISE

1. Translate, fill in the *i'raab* and analyze the following sentences.

i. قضيت الدين ثلثه

ii. سرني الخادم أمانته

iii. ذهب السياح أكثرهم إلى الوادي

iv. سطع القمر نوره

v. سرتنا الشوارع نظافتها

vi. قدم الأمير الوزير

vii. عاملت التاجر زيدا

viii. تمزق الكتاب غلافه

ix. أغلقت عائشة البستان بابه

x. كان أبو حامد الغزالي مجددا

104

<u>Section 3.10.4</u>
Conjunction – اَلْعَطْفُ بِحَرْفٍ/عَطْفُ النَّسَقِ

<u>Definition</u>: It is a تَابِعٌ which appears after a حَرْفُ عَطْفٍ. The حَرْفُ عَطْفٍ appears between the تَابِعٌ and the مَتْبُوعٌ. The meaning of the عَامِلٌ applicable to the مَتْبُوعٌ is also applicable to the تَابِعٌ.

- The تَابِعٌ is called مَعْطُوفٌ and the مَتْبُوعٌ is called مَعْطُوفٌ عَلَيْهِ.

    e.g.   جَاءَ زَيْدٌ وَعَمْرٌو   Zayd and 'Amr came.

عَمْرٌو	وَ	زَيْدٌ	جَاءَ
مَعْطُوفٌ	+	حَرْفُ عَطْفٍ	+	مَعْطُوفٌ عَلَيْهِ	

فِعْلٌ + فَاعِلٌ = جُمْلَةٌ فِعْلِيَّةٌ خَبَرِيَّةٌ

حُرُوفُ الْعَطْفِ:

The various حُرُوفُ عَطْفٍ are as follows:

وَ   فَ   ثُمَّ   حَتَّى   إِمَّا   أَوْ   أَمْ   لَا   بَلْ   لَكِنْ

Their details are as follows:

وَ (and): It is merely used for conjunction without regard to sequence.

    e.g.   جَاءَ زَيْدٌ وَبَكْرٌ   Zayd and Bakr came.

    Here, sequence is not considered.

فَ (then, thus):

- It conveys the meaning of sequence (تَرْتِيبٌ).

    e.g.   جَاءَ زَيْدٌ فَبَكْرٌ   Zayd came. Then, Bakr (came).

- It can also convey the meaning of causality (سَبَبِيَّةٌ).

    e.g.   أَنْزَلَ مِنَ السَّمَاءِ مَاءً فَتُصْبِحُ الْأَرْضُ مُخْضَرَّةً

    He sends down water from the sky. Therefore, the earth becomes green.

ثُمَّ (then): It conveys the meaning of sequence with delay.

    e.g.   جَاءَ زَيْدٌ ثُمَّ بَكْرٌ   Zayd came. Then, (after some time) Bakr (came).

حَتَّى (upto, till, even): It conveys the meaning of end point (غَايَةٌ).

    e.g.   قَرَأْتُ الْقُرْآنَ حَتَّى أَخِرَهُ   I read the Qur'an until the end.

    قَدِمَ الْحُجَّاجُ حَتَّى الْمُشَاةُ   The pilgrims came, even those on foot.

إِمَّا (either…or):

e.g.   اَلثَّمَرُ إِمَّا حُلْوٌ وَإِمَّا مُرٌّ   The fruit is either sweet or bitter.

أَوْ (or):

e.g.   لَبِثْنَا يَوْمًا أَوْ بَعْضَ يَوْمٍ   We stayed for a day or a part of a day.

أَمْ (or): It is generally used with an interrogative (اِسْتِفْهَامٌ).

e.g.   أَزَيْدٌ عِنْدَكَ اَمْ بَكْرٌ؟   Is Zayd with you or Bakr?

لَا (not): This negates from the مَعْطُوفٌ that which has been established for the مَعْطُوفٌ عَلَيْهِ.

e.g.   جَاءَنِي زَيْدٌ لَا بَكْرٌ   Zayd came to me and not Bakr.

بَلْ (but, instead, rather): It is used for إِضْرَابٌ i.e. to give up one notion for another.

- If it appears after a positive sentence (إِيجَابٌ) or a command (أَمْرٌ), it negates the ruling for that which is before it, and affirms it for that which is after it.

  e.g.   جَاءَنِي زَيْدٌ بَلْ بَكْرٌ   Zayd came to me. Rather, Bakr (came).

- If it appears after a (نَفْيٌ) or a (نَهْيٌ), it confirms this ruling (of negation) for the one before it, and affirms its opposite (i.e. opposite of negation) for the one after it.

  e.g.   مَا قَرَأْتُ الْكِتَابَ كُلَّهُ بَلْ بَعْضَهُ   I did not read the whole book; rather, [I read] some of it.

لٰكِنْ (but, however): It is generally used with a نَفْيٌ and serves the purpose of اِسْتِدْرَاكٌ i.e. to rectify.

e.g.   مَا جَاءَنِي زَيْدٌ لٰكِنْ بَكْرٌ جَاءَ   Zayd did not come to me but Bakr came.

Notes:

1. If the مَعْطُوفٌ عَلَيْهِ is a ضَمِيرٌ مَرْفُوعٌ مُتَّصِلٌ, then its ضَمِيرٌ مُنْفَصِلٌ has to be mentioned after it.

   e.g.   ضَرَبْتُ أَنَا وَزَيْدٌ   Zayd and I hit.

2. However, if after the ضَمِيرٌ مَرْفُوعٌ مُتَّصِلٌ, another word appears before the مَعْطُوفٌ, then the ضَمِيرٌ مُنْفَصِلٌ need not be mentioned.

   e.g.   ضَرَبْتُ الْيَوْمَ وَزَيْدٌ   Zayd and I hit, today.

       مَا أَشْرَكْنَا وَلَا أَبَاؤُنَا   Neither us nor our forefathers associated partners.

3. If the مَعْطُوفٌ عَلَيْهِ is a ضَمِيرٌ preceded by a حَرْفُ جَرٍّ, then the مَعْطُوفٌ should also be preceded by the same حَرْفُ جَرٍّ.

   e.g.   مَرَرْتُ بِكَ وَبِزَيْدٍ   I passed by you and Zayd.

EXERCISE

1. Fill in a suitable حَرْفُ عَطْفٍ, translate, fill in the *i'raab* and analyze the following sentences.

i. أتفاحا أكلت _____ عنبا؟

ii. قدمت إليه الطعام _____ ما أكله

iii. ما قابلته _____ قابلت وكيله

iv. باع عقاره _____ منزله

v. صلى الإمام _____ المأموم

vi. أأنت فعلت هذا _____ زبير؟

<u>Section 3.10.5</u>

عَطْفُ الْبَيَانِ

<u>Definition:</u> It is a تَابِعٌ which clarifies or specifies its مَتْبُوعٌ.

- Often, it is a more famous name of two names.

Example: قَامَ أَبُو حَفْصٍ عُمَرُ Abu Hafs ʿUmar stood up.

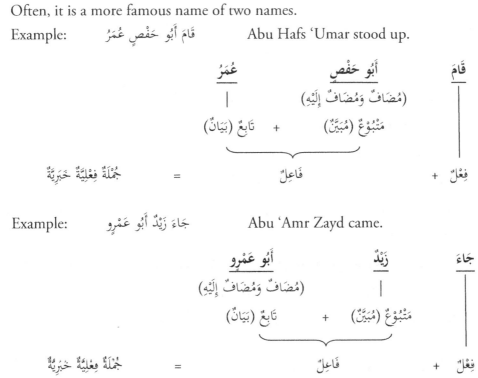

Example: جَاءَ زَيْدٌ أَبُو عَمْرٍو Abu ʿAmr Zayd came.

EXERCISE

1. Translate, fill in the *i'raab* and analyze the following sentences.

i. قام علي زين العابدين   ii. جعل الله الكعبة البيت الحرام قياما للناس

CHAPTER 4

اَلْعَوَامِلُ – Governing words

Definition: An عَامِلٌ is a word that governs/causes *i'raab* changes in another word.

There are two types of عَوَامِلُ: (1 مَعْنَوِيٌّ (2 لَفْظِيٌّ

1. عَامِلٌ مَعْنَوِيٌّ: It is an عَامِلٌ which is not in word form i.e. it is abstract.

   There are two types of عَامِلٌ مَعْنَوِيٌّ.

   i. اَلْاِبْتِدَاءُ: It means that being free of a عَامِلٌ لَفْظِيٌّ gives a مُبْتَدَأٌ رَفْعٌ.

      e.g.   زَيْدٌ قَائِمٌ   Zayd is standing.

      Here, زَيْدٌ is the مُبْتَدَأٌ, which is مَرْفُوعٌ because of اِبْتِدَاءٌ. قَائِمٌ is the خَبَرٌ and it is also مَرْفُوعٌ because of اِبْتِدَاءٌ.

   ii. In the case of فِعْلٌ مُضَارِعٌ, being free of a حَرْفُ جَزْمٍ or حَرْفُ نَصْبٍ gives a رَفْعٌ.

      e.g.   يَعْمَلُ زَيْدٌ   Zayd is working.

      Here يَعْمَلُ is مَرْفُوعٌ because it is free of any حَرْفُ جَزْمٍ or حَرْفُ نَصْبٍ.

2. عَامِلٌ لَفْظِيٌّ: It is an عَامِلٌ which is in word form.

   There are three types of عَامِلٌ لَفْظِيٌّ.

   i. اَلْحُرُوفُ
   ii. اَلْأَفْعَالُ
   iii. اَلْأَسْمَاءُ

Section 4.1

اَلْحُرُوْفُ الْعَامِلَةُ – Governing particles

A. Particles that govern *isms*

1.	اَلْحُرُوْفُ الْجَارَّةُ	refer to section 1.7
2.	اَلْحُرُوْفُ الْمُشَبَّهَةُ بِالْفِعْلِ	refer to section 1.8
3.	مَا وَلَا اَلْمُشَبَّهَتَانِ بِ لَيْسَ	refer to section 3.7.3
4.	وَاوُ الْمَعِيَّةِ	refer to section 3.8.4
5.	حُرُوْفُ الْإِسْتِثْنَاءِ	refer to section 3.8.8
6.	حُرُوْفُ النِّدَاءِ	refer to section 3.8.1
7.	لَا الَّتِي لِنَفْيِ الْجِنْسِ	refer to section 3.7.4

B. Particles that govern فِعْلٌ مُضَارِعٌ

1. اَلْحُرُوْفُ النَّاصِبَةُ

2. اَلْحُرُوْفُ الْجَازِمَةُ

<u>Section 4.1.1</u>[58]

اَلْحُرُوْفُ النَّاصِبَةُ – Particles that cause *nasb*

These are as follows: أَنْ   لَنْ   كَيْ   إِذَنْ

- These appear before فِعْلٌ مُضَارِعٌ and cause the following changes at the end:

  - They give the last letter a *fathah* if it is not a نُوْنٌ of تَثْنِيَةٌ or جَمْعٌ.

  - If the last letter is a نُوْنٌ of تَثْنِيَةٌ or جَمْعٌ, it is dropped. The exception is the نُوْنٌ of the two جَمْعٌ مُؤَنَّثٌ.

Table 4.1
اَلْحُرُوْفُ النَّاصِبَةُ

حَرْفُ نَصْبٍ	Meaning	Example	
أَنْ	that, to	أُرِيْدُ أَنْ أَدْخُلَ الْجَنَّةَ	I want to enter Paradise.
لَنْ	will not, never	لَنْ يَدْخُلَ الْكَافِرُ الْجَنَّةَ	The disbeliever will never enter Paradise.
كَيْ	so that	جِئْتُ كَيْ أَسْتَرِيْحَ	I came so I could rest.
إِذَنْ	then, in that case	إِذَنْ تَفُوْزَ فِي عَمَلِكَ	In that case, you will be successful in your work. [This is said in response to the one who may have said: أَجْتَهِدُ (I will work hard).]

Notes:

1. Sometimes أَنْ, together with its فِعْلٌ, gives the meaning of a مَصْدَرٌ. In this case, أَنْ is called أَنْ اَلْمَصْدَرِيَّةُ.

   صَوْمُكُمْ خَيْرٌ لَكُمْ   i.e.   أَنْ تَصُوْمُوْا خَيْرٌ لَكُمْ   e.g.
   Your fasting is better for you.

2. أَنْ is hidden after the following six حُرُوْفٌ and causes فِعْلٌ مُضَارِعٌ to be *mansoob*.[59]

   a. After حَتَّى:

   سِرْتُ حَتَّى أَدْخُلَ الْبَلَدَ   (حَتَّى أَنْ أَدْخُلَ)   e.g.
   I travelled until I entered the city.

---

[58] For more examples and exercises, please refer to *al-Nahw al-Wadih, Ibtida'iyyah*, vol. 1, 47-52.

[59] For more examples and exercises, please refer to *al-Nahw al-Wadih, Ibtida'iyyah*, vol. 2, 52-62.

b. After لَامُ الْمَنْفِيَّةِ or لَامُ الْجُحُودِ :لَامُ النَّفْي i.e. that لَامٌ which appears after كَانَ.

e.g. (لِأَنْ يُعَذِّبَهُمْ)   مَا كَانَ اللهُ لِيُعَذِّبَهُمْ

Allah was not going to punish them.

c. After أَوْ which has the meaning of إِلَى أَنْ (until) or إِلَّا أَنْ (but that/unless).

e.g. (إِلَى أَنْ تُعْطِيَنِي)   لَأُلْزَمَنَّكَ أَوْ تُعْطِيَنِي حَقِّي

I will not leave you until you give me my right.

(إِلَّا أَنْ يَعْتَذِرَ)   يُعَاقَبُ الْمُسِيْءُ أَوْ يَعْتَذِرَ

The sinner will be punished unless he provides an excuse.

d. After وَاوُ الصَّرْفِ :وَاوٌ i.e., a وَاوٌ that "turns away" from the word after it the effect which the عَامِلٌ had on the word before it (before the وَاوٌ).

e.g. (وَأَنْ تَكْذِبَ)   لَا تَأْمُرْ بِالصِّدْقِ وَتَكْذِبَ

Do not command the truth while you lie.

(Here, the وَاوٌ turned away/stopped the effect of لَا from تَكْذِبَ.)

- This وَاوٌ is also known as وَاوُ الْمُصَاحَبَةِ or وَاوُ الْمَعِيَّةِ.
- The sentence must start with a نَفْيٌ or نَهْيٌ.

e. After لَامُ التَّعْلِيلِ :لَامٌ i.e., a لَامٌ that has the meaning of كَيْ (it is also called لَامُ كَيْ).

e.g. (لِأَنْ أَسْتَرِيْحَ)   جِئْتُ لِأَسْتَرِيْحَ

I came so I could rest.

f. After الْفَاءُ السَّبَبِيَّةُ/الْجَوَابِيَّةُ :ف i.e., a ف that comes in the جَزَاءٌ to any of the following six.

1. الْأَمْرُ   e.g.   (فَأَنْ أُكْرِمَكَ)   زُرْنِي فَأُكْرِمَكَ

Visit me so that I treat you hospitably.

2. النَّهْيُ   e.g.   لَا تَطْغَوْا فِيْهِ فَيَحِلَّ عَلَيْكُمْ غَضَبِي

Do not cross the limit regarding it, lest My wrath descends upon you.

3. النَّفْيُ   e.g.   مَا تَزُوْرُنَا فَنُكْرِمَكَ

You do not visit us, otherwise we would have treated you hospitably.

4. الْاِسْتِفْهَامُ   e.g.   أَيْنَ بَيْتُكَ فَأَزُوْرَكَ

Where is your house, so I can visit you.

112

5. اَلتَّمَنِّي e.g. لَيْتَ لِيْ مَالًا فَأُنْفِقَهُ

I wish I had wealth, so I would have spent it.

6. اَلْعَرْضُ e.g. أَلَا تَنْزِلُ بِنَا فَتُصِيْبَ خَيْرًا

Why don't you visit us so that you receive good!

3. أَنْ has to be written after a لَامُ التَّعْلِيْلِ if the لَامُ التَّعْلِيْلِ is joined to a لَاءٌ نَافِيَةٌ.

e.g. لِئَلَّا يَعْلَمَ (لِأَنْ لَا) So that he does not know.

4. أَنْ which appears after a فِعْلٌ with the root letters ع – ل – م is not a حَرْفُ نَصْبٍ. Therefore, it does not cause فِعْلٌ مُضَارِعٌ to be *mansoob*. Such an أَنْ is known as أَنْ الْمُخَفَّفَةُ مِنَ الْمُثَقَّلَةِ i.e., that أَنْ which was أَنَّ.

e.g. عَلِمْتُ أَنْ سَيَقُوْمُ I knew that he will stand up.

e.g. عَلِمَ أَنْ سَيَكُوْنُ مِنْكُمْ مَرْضَى He knew that some of you will be sick.

EXERCISE

1. Translate, fill in the *i'raab* and point out the حَرْفُ نَصْبٍ and its effect in the following sentences.

i. يجتهد الطالب لينجح

ii. لن يفوز الكسلان

iii. جئت كي أتعلم

iv. لم يكن الشرطي ليسرق

v. لا تأكل حتى تجوع

vi. إن الله يأمركم أن تذبحوا بقرة

vii. اصنع المعروف فتنال الشكر

viii. فأراد ربك أن يبلغا أشدهما ويستخرجا كنزهما

113

<u>Section 4.1.2</u>[60]

اَلْحُرُوفُ الْجَازِمَةُ – Particles that cause *jazm*

These are as follows: لَاءُ النَّهْي   لَامُ الْأَمْرِ   لَمَّا   لَمْ   إِنْ

- These appear before فِعْلٌ مُضَارِعٌ and cause the following changes at the end:
  - They give the last letter a *sukoon* if it is not a نُوْنٌ of تَثْنِيَةٌ or جَمْعٌ.
  - If the last letter is a نُوْنٌ of تَثْنِيَةٌ or جَمْعٌ, it will be dropped. The exception is the نُوْنٌ of the two جَمْعٌ مُؤَنَّثٌ.

Table 4.2
اَلْحُرُوفُ الْجَازِمَةُ

حَرْفُ جَزْم	Meaning	Example	
إِنْ	if	إِنْ تَجْلِسْ أَجْلِسْ	If you sit, I will sit.
لَمْ	did not	لَمْ يَضْرِبْنِيْ	He did not hit me.
لَمَّا	not yet	ذَهَبَ الْوَلَدُ وَ لَمَّا يَعُدْ	The boy went but has not returned yet.
لِ	should, shall, let	لِيَجْلِسْ	He should sit.
لَا	do not	لَا تَجْلِسْ	Do not sit.

Notes:

1. إِنْ appears before two verbal sentences. The first one is called شَرْطٌ (condition) and the second جَزَاءٌ (answer/result).

2. If إِنْ appears before إِلَّا, it should be translated negatively.

   e.g.   إِنْ هٰذَا إِلَّا مَلَكٌ كَرِيْمٌ   He is <u>not</u> but an honorable angel.

   <u>Note</u>: This negation could also be expressed as "He is only an honorable angel."

3. لَمْ can also be used to give the meaning of لَمَّا. For this, بَعْدُ or إِلَى الآنَ is added after the فِعْلٌ مُضَارِعٌ which was given جَزْمٌ by لَمْ.

   e.g.   لَمْ يَذْهَبْ بَعْدُ   He has not gone yet.

4. فَ should be brought before the جَزَاءٌ of a شَرْطٌ when the جَزَاءٌ is one of the following:

   a. جُمْلَةٌ اِسْمِيَّةٌ   e.g.   إِنْ تَأْتِنِيْ فَأَنْتَ مُكْرَمٌ

      If you come to me you will be treated hospitably.

---

[60] For more examples and exercises, please refer to *al-Nahw al-Wadih, Ibtida'iyyah*, vol. 1, 52-57 & vol. 2, 63-66.

b.   أَمْرٌ   e.g.   إِنْ رَأَيْتَ زَيْدًا فَأَكْرِمْهُ

If you see Zayd, treat him hospitably.

c.   نَهْيٌ   e.g.   إِنْ أَتَاكَ زَيْدٌ فَلَا تُهِنْهُ

If Zayd comes to you, do not humiliate him.

d.   دُعَاءٌ   e.g.   إِنْ أَكْرَمْتَنِي فَجَزَاكَ اللهُ خَيْرًا

If you treat me hospitably, then, may Allah reward you well.

5.   اَلْفِعْلُ الْمَاضِيْ will be translated in the future tense when it is…

   a.   used as a دُعَاءٌ   e.g.   جَزَاكَ اللهُ خَيْرًا

                            May Allah reward you well.

   b.   preceded by حَرْفُ شَرْطٍ   e.g.   إِنْ جَلَسْتَ جَلَسْتُ

                            If you sit, I will sit.

   c.   preceded by اِسْمٌ مَوْصُوْلٌ   e.g.   مَنْ جَاءَ بِالْحَسَنَةِ فَلَهُ عَشْرُ أَمْثَالِهَا

                            Whoever comes with good, there will be ten like it for him.

EXERCISE

1. Translate, fill in the *i'raab* and point out the حَرْفُ جَزْمٍ and its effect on the following sentences.

iv. كَبِرَ الغلام ولما يتهذب	i. ليفتح علي النافذة
v. إن يسافر أخوك أسافر معه	ii. لا تكثر من الضحك
vi. إن تنصروا الله ينصركم	iii. اختلف الشريكان ولم يتفقا

Section 4.2
اَلْأَفْعَالُ الْعَامِلَةُ – Governing *fi'l*s

Section 4.2.1
__اَلْفِعْلُ الْمَعْرُوْفُ – Active *fi'l*:__ It is a فِعْلٌ whose doer is known/mentioned.

- فِعْلٌ مَعْرُوْفٌ, whether transitive or intransitive, governs the following *isms*, as and when applicable:
    - it gives رَفْعٌ to the فَاعِلٌ.
    - it gives نَصْبٌ to the following, as and when applicable:
        i. مَفْعُوْلٌ بِهِ (can only be governed by a اَلْفِعْلُ الْمُتَعَدِّيْ)
        ii. مَفْعُوْلٌ مُطْلَقٌ
        iii. مَفْعُوْلٌ مَعَهُ
        iv. مَفْعُوْلٌ لَهُ
        v. مَفْعُوْلٌ فِيْهِ
        vi. حَالٌ
        vii. تَمْيِيْزٌ

Section 4.2.2
__اَلْفِعْلُ الْمَجْهُوْلُ – Passive *fi'l*:__ It is a فِعْلٌ whose doer is not known/mentioned.

- فِعْلٌ مَجْهُوْلٌ is also known as فِعْلٌ مَا لَمْ يُسَمَّ فَاعِلُهُ (a فِعْلٌ whose فَاعِلٌ is not named).
- It gives رَفْعٌ to the نَائِبُ فَاعِلٍ (originally the مَفْعُوْلٌ بِهِ).
- It gives نَصْبٌ to all the remaining مَنْصُوْبَاتٌ.
- e.g. ضُرِبَ زَيْدٌ يَوْمَ الْجُمُعَةِ أَمَامَ الْقَاضِيْ ضَرْبًا شَدِيْدًا فِيْ دَارِهِ تَأْدِيْبًا

    Zayd was beaten severely on Friday, in front of the Judge, in his office/house, to teach him manners.

Section 4.2.3
__اَلْفِعْلُ اللَّازِمُ – Intransitive *fi'l*:__ It is a فِعْلٌ whose meaning can be understood without a مَفْعُوْلٌ بِهِ.

- e.g.　جَلَسَ زَيْدٌ　　Zayd sat.

Section 4.2.4
__اَلْأَفْعَالُ النَّاقِصَةُ:__ These were discussed earlier in section 1.9.

<u>Section 4.2.5</u>[61]

اَلْفِعْلُ الْمُتَعَدِّي – Transitive *fi'l*

<u>Definition:</u> It is a فِعْلٌ whose meaning cannot be understood without a مَفْعُولٌ بِهِ.

e.g.   ضَرَبَ زَيْدٌ بَكْرًا   Zayd hit Bakr.

There are four types of اَلْفِعْلُ الْمُتَعَدِّي. These are as follows:

1. Those *fi'l*s which require one مَفْعُولٌ بِهِ as is the case with most *muta'addi* verbs.

    e.g.   ضَرَبَ زَيْدٌ بَكْرًا

2. Those *fi'l*s which **can** be given two مَفْعُولٌ بِهِ. These include the following:

    ▪ Any فِعْلٌ which has the meaning of إِعْطَاءٌ (to give).

    e.g.   أَعْطَى   مَنَحَ   وَهَبَ   etc.

    أَعْطَيْتُ السَّائِلَ خُبْزًا I gave the beggar a bread.

    ▪ Some other *fi'l*s which can also have two مَفْعُولٌ بِهِ include the following

    أَمَرَ   كَسَى   سَأَلَ   etc.

    e.g.   يَكْسُو الْعِلْمُ أَهْلَهُ وَقَارًا   Knowledge clothes its possessor with dignity.

3. Those *fi'l*s which **must** be given two اَلْمَفْعُولُ بِهِ.

    ▪ These *fi'l*s are known as أَفْعَالُ الْقُلُوبِ (*fi'l*s which relate to the heart/feelings).

    ▪ They enter upon a مُبْتَدَأً and خَبَرٌ unlike the *fi'l*s above (number 2).

Table 4.3
أَفْعَالُ الْقُلُوبِ

Fi'l	Usage	Example	
رَأَى	used for certainty (يَقِيْنٌ)	رَأَيْتُ سَعِيْدًا ذَاهِبًا	I was sure Sa'eed was going.
وَجَدَ	used for certainty (يَقِيْنٌ)	وَجَدْتُ رَشِيْدًا عَالِمًا	I was sure Rasheed was knowledgeable.
عَلِمَ	used for certainty (يَقِيْنٌ)	عَلِمْتُ زَيْدًا أَمِيْنًا	I was sure Zayd was trustworthy.
زَعَمَ	used for certainty (يَقِيْنٌ) or doubt (شَكٌّ)	زَعَمْتُ زَيْدًا حَاضِرًا	I was sure Zayd was present. / I thought Zayd was present.
حَسِبَ	used for doubt (شَكٌّ)	حَسِبْتُ زَيْدًا فَاضِلًا	I thought Zayd was well-educated.
خَالَ	used for doubt (شَكٌّ)	خِلْتُ خَالِدًا قَائِمًا	I thought Khalid was standing.
ظَنَّ	used for doubt (شَكٌّ)	ظَنَنْتُ بَكْرًا نَائِمًا	I thought Bakr was sleeping.

---

[61] For more details, examples, and exercises, please refer to *al-Nahw al-Wadih, Ibtida'iyyah*, vol. 3, 69-71.

<u>Note:</u> Other *fi'ls* which also require two مَفْعُوْلٌ بِهِ include the following:

صَيَّرَ   to make something something else

e.g.   صَيَّرْتُ الْأَوْرَاقَ كِتَابًا I made the pages a book.

اِتَّخَذَ   to take someone/something as someone/something

e.g.   وَاتَّخَذَ اللهُ إِبْرَاهِيْمَ خَلِيْلًا Allah took Ibraheem (peace be upon him) as a friend.

جَعَلَ   to make something something else

e.g.   جَعَلْتُ الْكِتَابَ مُرَتَّبًا I made the book organized.

4. Those *fi'ls* which require three مَفْعُوْلٌ بِهِ. Each of these has the meaning of "informing" or "showing." These are as follows:

Table 4.4

Fi'l		Example
أَرَى	أَرَيْتُ زَيْدًا خَالِدًا نَائِمًا	I informed Zayd that Khalid is sleeping.
أَعْلَمَ	أَعْلَمْتُ زَيْدًا بَكْرًا فَاضِلًا	I informed Zayd that Bakr is well-educated.
أَنْبَأَ	أَنْبَأَنِي الرَّسُوْلُ الْأَمِيْرَ قَادِمًا	The messenger informed me that the chief is coming.
نَبَّأَ	نَبَّأْتُهُمُ الْكِبْرَ مَمْقُوْتًا	I informed them that arrogance is hated.
أَخْبَرَ	أَخْبَرْتُ الْغِلْمَانَ اللَّعْبَ مُفِيْدًا	I informed the boys that sport is beneficial.
خَبَّرَ	خَبَّرْتُ الْمُسَافِرِيْنَ الْقِطَارَ مُتَأَخِّرًا	I informed the travellers that the train is late.
حَدَّثَ	حَدَّثْتُ الْأَوْلَادَ السِّبَاحَةَ نَافِعَةً	I informed the children that swimming is beneficial.

EXERCISE

1. Translate, fill in the *i'raab* and analyze the following sentences.

i. نبأت سعيدا أخاه قادما   iv. رأيت الصلح خيرا

ii. أعطيت زيدا درهما   v. أخبرني زيد أباه مريضا

iii. فهم سعيد الدرس   vi. ظننت الجو معتدلا

118

Section 4.2.6[62]
أَفْعَالُ الْمُقَارَبَةِ وَالرَّجَاءِ وَالشُّرُوعِ

Definition: These *fiʿl*s are actually a type of أَفْعَالٌ نَاقِصَةٌ and they behave the same way. They also enter upon مُبْتَدَأٌ & خَبَرٌ and give رَفْعٌ to their اِسْمٌ and نَصْبٌ to their خَبَرٌ. The difference is that their خَبَرٌ is always جُمْلَةٌ فِعْلِيَّةٌ.

They are used for the following purposes:

1. أَفْعَالُ الْمُقَارَبَةِ show nearness in the attainment (حُصُولٌ) of the خَبَرٌ.
2. أَفْعَالُ الرَّجَاءِ show desire for attainment of خَبَرٌ.
3. أَفْعَالُ الشُّرُوعِ show commencement of action.

Table 4.5
أَفْعَالُ الْمُقَارَبَةِ وَالرَّجَاءِ وَالشُّرُوعِ

فِعْلٌ	اِسْمٌ	خَبَرٌ	Type	Example	
كَادَ	مَرْفُوعٌ	مُضَارِعٌ preferably without أَنْ	حُصُولٌ	كَادَ زَيْدٌ يَذْهَبُ	Zayd was about to go.
كَرَبَ/كَرُبَ*	مَرْفُوعٌ	مُضَارِعٌ preferably without أَنْ	حُصُولٌ	كَرَبَ خَالِدٌ يَجْلِسُ	Khalid was about to sit.
أَوْشَكَ	مَرْفُوعٌ	مُضَارِعٌ preferably with أَنْ	حُصُولٌ	أَوْشَكَ زَيْدٌ أَنْ يَجْلِسَ	Zayd was about to sit.
عَسَى*	مَرْفُوعٌ	مُضَارِعٌ preferably with أَنْ	رَجَاءٌ	عَسَى زَيْدٌ أَنْ يَخْرُجَ	Hopefully Zayd will come out.
طَفِقَ*	مَرْفُوعٌ	مُضَارِعٌ without أَنْ	شُرُوعٌ	طَفِقَ زَيْدٌ يَكْتُبُ	Zayd began writing.
جَعَلَ*	مَرْفُوعٌ	مُضَارِعٌ without أَنْ	شُرُوعٌ	جَعَلَ زَيْدٌ يَقْرَأُ	Zayd began reading.
أَخَذَ*	مَرْفُوعٌ	مُضَارِعٌ without أَنْ	شُرُوعٌ	أَخَذَ زَيْدٌ يَأْكُلُ	Zayd began eating.

* These *fiʿl*s are used only in past tense.

- The أَفْعَالُ الشُّرُوعِ can be used as normal *fiʿl*s too.

  e.g.   أَخَذَ زَيْدٌ ثَوْبَهُ   Zayd took his clothes.

---

[62] For more details, examples and exercises, please refer to *al-Nahw al-Wadih*, Thanawiyyah, vol. 1, 103-108.

<u>Sentence Analysis:</u> عَسَى زَيْدٌ أَنْ يَخْرُجَ Hopefully Zayd will come out.

أَنْ يَخْرُجَ	زَيْدٌ	عَسَى
أَنْ مصدرية + فِعْلٌ + فَاعِلٌ (هُوَ)		

خَبَرُ عَسَى   اِسْمُ عَسَى   فِعْلُ الرَّجَاءِ

EXERCISE

1. Translate, fill in the *i'raab* and analyze the following sentences.

    iv. أوشك أن يفتح باب المدرسة   i. عسى الله أن يشفيك

    v. أخذت أكتب   ii. تكاد السموات يتفطرن

    vi. جعل زيد يمسح رأسه   iii. عست المرأة أن تقوم

أَفْعَالُ الْمَدْحِ وَالذَّمِّ – *Fiʿls* of praise and blame

Fiʿls of praise:	نِعْمَ	e.g.	نِعْمَ الرَّجُلُ زَيْدٌ	What a wonderful man Zayd is!
	حَبَّذَا	e.g.	حَبَّذَا زَيْدٌ	What a wonderful man Zayd is!
Fiʿls of blame:	بِئْسَ	e.g.	بِئْسَ الرَّجُلُ زَيْدٌ	What an evil man Zayd is!
	سَاءَ	e.g.	سَاءَ الرَّجُلُ زَيْدٌ	What an evil man Zayd is!

- That which appears after the فَاعِلٌ is called مَخْصُوصٌ بِالذَّمِّ or مَخْصُوصٌ بِالْمَدْحِ.

- The فَاعِلٌ of سَاءَ – بِئْسَ – نِعْمَ must be one of the following:

    i. prefixed with ال.

    e.g. نِعْمَ الرَّجُلُ زَيْدٌ   What a wonderful man Zayd is!

    ii. مُضَافٌ to an اِسْمٌ prefixed with ال.

    e.g. نِعْمَ صَاحِبُ الْعِلْمِ زَيْدٌ   What a wonderful learned man Zayd is!

    iii. a hidden ضَمِيرٌ followed by a نَكِرَةٌ مَنْصُوبَةٌ (being تَمْيِيزٌ).

    e.g. [نِعْمَ (هُوَ) رَجُلًا زَيْدٌ]   نِعْمَ رَجُلًا زَيْدٌ   What a wonderful man Zayd is!

    iv. The word مَا.

    e.g. بِئْسَ مَا كَانُوا يَفْعَلُونَ   How evil is what they used to do!

In حَبَّذَا زَيْدٌ,   حَبَّ is the فِعْلٌ.

        ذَا (اِسْمُ إِشَارَةٍ) is its فَاعِلٌ.

        زَيْدٌ is the مَخْصُوصٌ بِالْمَدْحِ.

Notes:

1. These *fiʿls* are used in the past tense in their singular form (masculine or feminine).

2. At times the مَخْصُوصٌ بِالْمَدْحِ is dropped.

    e.g. نِعْمَ الْعَبْدُ   i.e. نِعْمَ الْعَبْدُ أَيُّوبُ   What a wonderful slave Ayyub is!

---

[63] For more details, examples and exercises, please refer to *al-Nahw al-Wadih*, *Thanawiyyah*, vol. 1, 57-59.

Sentence Analysis:

نِعْمَ الرَّجُلُ زَيْدٌ

فِعْلُ الْمَدْحِ + فَاعِلٌ + مَخْصُوصٌ بِالْمَدْحِ

خَبَرٌ مُقَدَّمٌ

جُمْلَةٌ اِسْمِيَّةٌ خَبَرِيَّةٌ = مُبْتَدَأٌ مُؤَخَّرٌ

EXERCISE

1. Translate, fill in the *i'raab* and analyze the following sentences.

  i.   نعمت الابنة فاطمة

  ii.   حبذا الاتفاق

  iii.   نعم المولى

122

<u>Section 4.2.8</u>[64]

<u>أَفْعَالُ التَّعَجُّب – *Fi'ls* of wonder</u>

For three-letter *fi'ls* (اَلثُّلَاثِيُّ الْمُجَرَّدُ), there are two *wazns* for expressing wonder or amazement.

1. مَا أَفْعَلَهُ: مَا has the meaning of أَيُّ شَيْءٍ.

   e.g.   مَا أَحْسَنَ زَيْدًا   How wonderful Zayd is!

$$\underset{\text{فِعْلٌ + فَاعِلٌ (هُوَ)}}{\underline{\text{أَحْسَنَ}}} + \underset{\text{مَفْعُوْلٌ بِهِ}}{\underline{\text{زَيْدًا}}} \qquad \qquad \underset{}{\underline{\text{مَا}}}$$

$$\underset{}{\text{مُبْتَدَأٌ}} + \underset{\text{خَبَرٌ (جُمْلَةٌ فِعْلِيَّةٌ خَبَرِيَّةٌ)}}{} = \text{جُمْلَةٌ اِسْمِيَّةٌ إِنْشَائِيَّةٌ}$$

2. أَفْعِلْ بِهِ: أَفْعِلْ (فِعْلُ أَمْرٍ) has the meaning of past tense and the بِ is extra (زَائِدَةٌ).

   e.g.   أَحْسِنْ بِزَيْدٍ   (أَحْسَنَ زَيْدٌ)   How wonderful Zayd is!

   جُمْلَةٌ فِعْلِيَّةٌ إِنْشَائِيَّةٌ

- To express wonder for other than three-letter *fi'ls* (غَيْرُ الثُّلَاثِيِّ الْمُجَرَّدِ), a word such as أَشْدِدْ بِ/أَ، أَحْسِنْ بِ /مَا أَحْسَنَ or مَا أَشَدَّ etc. should be placed before the مَصْدَر of the desired فِعْلٌ. The مَصْدَر will be مَفْعُوْلٌ بِهِ, thus مَنْصُوْبٌ.

   e.g.   مَا أَشَدَّ إِكْرَامَ النَّاسِ لِلْعُلَمَاءِ   How very respectful people are towards the learned!

EXERCISE

1. Translate, fill in the i'raab and analyze the following sentences.

   i. أطول بزيد

   ii. ما أشد بياض شعره

   iii. ما أطول الرجلين

---

[64] For more details, examples and exercises, please refer to *al-Nahw al-Wadih*, *Thanawiyyah*, vol. 1, 60-63.

Section 4.3

اَلْأَسْمَاءُ الْعَامِلَةُ – Governing *isms*

Amongst these, أَسْمَاءُ الْأَفْعَالِ were discussed in section 2.4.4. Here, we will discuss the rest.

Section 4.3.1[65]

اَلْأَسْمَاءُ الشَّرْطِيَّةُ – Conditional *isms*

- They govern two فِعْلٌ مُضَارِعٌ giving both a جَزْمٌ.
- They appear before two sentences. The first is called شَرْطٌ (condition) and the second جَزَاءٌ (result).

Table 4.6
اَلْأَسْمَاءُ الشَّرْطِيَّةُ

Ism	Meaning	Usage		Example
1. مَنْ	who, whoever	لِلْعَاقِلِ	مَنْ يُكْرِمْنِيْ أُكْرِمْهُ	Whoever treats me hospitably, I will treat him hospitably.
2. مَا	what, whatever	لِغَيْرِ الْعَاقِلِ	مَا تَأْكُلْ أُكُلْ	Whatever you eat, I will eat.
3. مَهْمَا	however much	لِغَيْرِ الْعَاقِلِ	مَهْمَا تُنْفِقْ فِي الْخَيْرِ يَنْفَعْكَ	Whatever you spend in the way of good, will benefit you.
4. مَتَى	when	لِلزَّمَانِ	مَتَى تَذْهَبْ أَذْهَبْ	Whenever you go, I will go.
5. أَيَّانَ	when	لِلزَّمَانِ	أَيَّانَ تُسَافِرْ أُسَافِرْ	Whenever you travel, I will travel.
6. أَيْنَ	where	لِلْمَكَانِ	أَيْنَ تَذْهَبْ أَذْهَبْ	Wherever you go, I will go.
7. أَنَّى	where	لِلْمَكَانِ	أَنَّى تَنْزِلْ أَنْزِلْ	Wherever you stay, I will stay.
8. حَيْثُمَا	where	لِلْمَكَانِ	حَيْثُمَا تُسَافِرْ أُسَافِرْ	Wherever you travel, I will travel.
9. كَيْفَمَا	how, manner	لِلْحَالِ	كَيْفَمَا تَقْعُدْ أَقْعُدْ	Whichever way you sit, I will sit.
10. أَيٌّ	any of the above	any of the above	أَيُّ مَكَانٍ تَذْهَبْ أَذْهَبْ	Whichever place you go, I will go.

Notes:

1. إِنْ and إِذْمَا have the same function as اَلْأَسْمَاءُ الشَّرْطِيَّةُ i.e. giving *jazm* to two فِعْلٌ مُضَارِعٌ except that they are particles (حَرْفَا الشَّرْطِ) and not *isms*. Collectively they (*isms* and particles) are all called أَدَوَاتُ الشَّرْطِ الْجَازِمَةُ.

---

[65] For more examples and exercises, please refer to *al-Nahw al-Wadih*, *Ibtida'iyyah*, vol. 2, 66-71.

إنْ	if	e.g.	إنْ تَذْهَبْ أَذْهَبْ	If you go, I will go.
إذْمَا	if	e.g.	إذْمَا تَفْعَلْ شَرًّا تَنْدَمْ	If you do evil, you will be regretful.

2. There are other أَدَوَاتُ الشَّرْطِ that are غَيْرُ جَازِمَةٍ, i.e. they do not give جَزْمٌ to فِعْلٌ مُضَارِعٌ. Some of these are discussed in Section 4.4, # 13 (حُرُوْفُ الشَّرْطِ الَّتِيْ لَا تَجْزِمُ). Amongst the الْأَسْمَاءُ الشَّرْطِيَّةُ, which do not give جَزْمٌ, two are discussed below:

i. كُلَّمَا (whenever, every time)

This is a ظَرْفٌ, and enters upon فِعْلٌ مَاضٍ. It also conveys the meaning of emphasis and repetition.

e.g. كُلَّمَا مَرِضْتُ ذَهَبْتُ إِلَى الطَّبِيْبِ   Whenever I fell sick, I went to the doctor.

ii. إِذَا (when)

This is also a ظَرْفٌ, and is used to give the meaning of فِعْلٌ مُضَارِعٌ. It also entails the meaning of condition (مُتَضَمِّنٌ مَعْنَى الشَّرْطِ).

e.g. إِذَا لَقِيْتَهُ فَسَلِّمْ عَلَيْهِ   When you meet him, greet him.

3. When the following *isms* are used for اِسْتِفْهَامٌ (interrogative), they appear before one sentence.

أَيٌّ   أَنَّى   أَيْنَ   أَيَّانَ   مَتَى   مَا   مَنْ

e.g.   مَتَى تُسَافِرُ   أَيْنَ تَذْهَبُ   مَنْ أَنْتَ   مَا هَذَا

EXERCISE

1. Complete the following sentences with a suitable جَزَاءٌ.

i.	من يصنع معروفا _____	v.	أنى ينزل ذو العلم _____
ii.	ما تخف من أعمالك _____	vi.	متى تسافر _____
iii.	كيفما تعامل إخوانك _____	vii.	من احترم الناس _____
iv.	أيان يكثر فراغ الشباب _____	viii.	من يكثر كلامه _____

125

<u>Section 4.3.2</u>[66]

اِسْمُ الْفَاعِلِ – Active participle

<u>Definition:</u> It is an اِسْمٌ which indicates the one doing or undertaking an action described by the root letters. This is irrespective of its position in a sentence.

- It is created from ثُلَاثِيٌّ مُجَرَّدٌ *fi'ls* on the pattern of فَاعِلٌ. For other than ثُلَاثِيٌّ مُجَرَّدٌ *fi'ls*, it is created on the pattern of its مُضَارِعٌ by changing the حَرْفُ مُضَارِعٍ into a *meem* with a *dammah*, and giving a *kasrah* to the letter before the last.

<u>Effect:</u>

- It has the same effect as that of its active *fi'l* (فِعْلٌ مَعْرُوفٌ) i.e. if its فِعْلٌ is لَازِمٌ, it gives رَفْعٌ to the فَاعِلٌ; and if it is مُتَعَدٍّ, it gives رَفْعٌ to the فَاعِلٌ and نَصْبٌ to the مَفْعُولٌ بِهِ.

- اِسْمُ الْفَاعِلِ acts only in either of the following two situations:

1. When it is prefixed with ال.

    e.g.   أَنَا الشَّاكِرُ نِعْمَتَكَ   I am grateful for your favor.

2. When it indicates present or future tense and is preceded by مُبْتَدَأٌ or مَوْصُوفٌ or اِسْتِفْهَامٌ or نَفْيٌ. For example,

    a. مُبْتَدَأٌ   e.g.   زَيْدٌ ضَارِبٌ أَبُوهُ بَكْرًا   Zayd's father is beating/will beat Bakr.

    b. مَوْصُوفٌ   e.g.   مَرَرْتُ بِرَجُلٍ ضَارِبٍ أَبُوهُ بَكْرًا   I passed by a man whose father is beating/will beat Bakr.

    c. اِسْتِفْهَامٌ   e.g.   أَضَارِبٌ زَيْدٌ بَكْرًا؟   Is Zayd beating Bakr?/Will Zayd beat Bakr?

    d. نَفْيٌ   e.g.   مَا قَائِمٌ زَيْدٌ   Zayd is not standing/will not stand.

<u>Sentence Analysis:</u>

بَكْرًا	أَبُوهُ	ضَارِبٌ	زَيْدٌ
	(مُضَافٌ وَمُضَافٌ إِلَيْهِ)		
مَفْعُولُهُ +	فَاعِلُهُ +	اِسْمُ الْفَاعِلِ	
	خَبَرٌ		مُبْتَدَأٌ +
جُمْلَةٌ اِسْمِيَّةٌ خَبَرِيَّةٌ =			

---

[66] This section and the following sub-section are based on the discussion in *al-Nahw al-Wadih*. See *al-Nahw al-Wadih, Thanawiyyah*, vol. 2, 71-76.

126

<u>Section 4.3.2.1</u>

اِسْمُ الْمُبَالَغَةِ

<u>Definition:</u> It is an اِسْمٌ which conveys extremity/intensity in meaning.

- اِسْمُ الْفَاعِلِ is turned into the *seeghahs* of مُبَالَغَةٌ when exaggeration in meaning is intended.
- Some of the *wazns* of مُبَالَغَةٌ are as follows:

Table 4.7

أَوْزَانُ اِسْمِ الْمُبَالَغَةِ

Wazns	Examples	
	Arabic	Meaning
فَعِيلٌ	عَلِيمٌ	most learned
فَاعُوْلٌ	فَارُوْقٌ	great distinguisher
فَعَّالٌ	ضَحَّاكٌ	someone who laughs a lot
فَعُوْلٌ	صَبُوْرٌ	very patient
فَعُّوْلٌ	قَيُّوْمٌ	careful maintainer/sustainer
مِفْعِيْلٌ	مِنْطِيْقٌ	very eloquent
مِفْعَالٌ	مِعْوَانٌ	someone who helps frequently

- اِسْمُ الْمُبَالَغَةِ does the عَمَلٌ of اِسْمُ الْفَاعِلِ with the same conditions.

  e.g. يُعْجِبُنِي الشَّكُوْرُ الْمُنْعِمَ

  The one who is very grateful to the one who does good (to him), pleases me.

  إِنَّ الْجَبَانَ هَيَّابٌ لِقَاءَ الْعَدُوِّ

  Indeed, the coward is very scared of meeting the enemy.

<u>Notes:</u>

1. The round ة at the end of some *wazns* is for مُبَالَغَةٌ and not for gender.

   e.g. فَعَّالَةٌ   عَلَّامَةٌ   well-learned

2. The *wazn* فَعَّالٌ is also used to denote a profession.

   e.g. طَبَّاخٌ   cook   نَجَّارٌ   carpenter

   حَدَّادٌ   blacksmith   حَلَّاقٌ   barber

EXERCISES

1. Translate, fill in the *i'raab* and point out the effect and tense of the اِسْمُ الْفَاعِلِ in the following sentences.

i.   أذاهب صديقنا؟   v.   ما شارب زيد القهوة

ii.   الضارب زيد بكرا   vi.   زيد شارب القهوة

iii.   لست بجاحد فضلكم   vii.   المؤمن محسن عمله

iv.   أمنجز أنتم وعدكم؟   viii.   الطالب قارئ كتابا

<u>**Section 4.3.3**</u>[67]

اِسْمُ الْمَفْعُوْل – Passive participle

<u>**Definition:**</u> It is an اِسْمٌ which indicates the one upon whom an action described by the root letters is done. This is irrespective of its position in a sentence.

- It is created from ثُلَاثِيٌّ مُجَرَّدٌ fi'ls on the pattern of مَفْعُوْلٌ. For other than ثُلَاثِيٌّ مُجَرَّدٌ, it is created on the pattern of its مُضَارِعٌ by changing the حَرْفُ مُضَارِعٍ into a *meem* with a *dammah*, and giving a *fathah* to the letter before the last.

<u>**Effect:**</u>

- It has the same effect as that of its passive fi'l (فِعْلٌ مَجْهُوْلٌ), i.e. it gives رَفْعٌ to the نَائِبُ الْفَاعِلِ.
- The rules mentioned above regarding the اِسْمُ الْفَاعِلِ also apply here.

Examples:

i. prefixed with *alif-laam*	e.g.	الْمُسَمَّى هِشَامًا أَخِيْ	The one named Hisham is my brother.
ii. مُبْتَدَأً	e.g.	زَيْدٌ مَضْرُوْبٌ اِبْنُهُ	Zayd's son is being beaten/will be beaten.
iii. مَوْصُوْفٌ	e.g.	مَرَرْتُ بِرَجُلٍ مَضْرُوْبٍ اِبْنُهُ	I passed by a man whose son is being beaten/will be beaten.
iv. اِسْتِفْهَامٌ	e.g.	أَمَضْرُوْبٌ زَيْدٌ؟	Is Zayd being beaten?/Will Zayd be beaten?
v. نَفْيٌ	e.g.	مَا مَضْرُوْبٌ زَيْدٌ	Zayd is not being beaten/will not be beaten.

EXERCISE

1. Translate, fill in the *i'raab* and point out the effect and tense of the اِسْمُ الْمَفْعُوْلِ in the following sentences.

iv. الفقير معطًى ثوباً

i. زيد مسموع خبره

v. الكتاب متقن طبعه

ii. خالد معلَّم ابنه الحياكة

vi. الأشجار مقطوعة أغصاتها

iii. العلم معروفة فوائده

---

[67] This section is based on the discussion in *al-Nahw al-Wadih*. See *al-Nahw al-Wadih, Thanawiyyah*, vol 2, 77-82.

<u>Section 4.3.4</u>[68]

اِسْمُ الْفَاعِلِ An adjective that is similar to – اَلصِّفَةُ الْمُشَبَّهَةُ بِاسْمِ الْفَاعِلِ

<u>Definition:</u> It is an اِسْمٌ which is created from the مَصْدَر of a اَلثُّلَاثِيُّ اللَّازِمُ (three-letter intransitive *fi'l*) to indicate permanent existence of the meaning in the doer.

- Like its فِعْلٌ لَازِمٌ, it generally gives the فَاعِلٌ a رَفْعٌ.

  e.g.   حَسَنٌ وَجْهُهُ   His face is beautiful.

- It conveys permanency of meaning in the object it relates to e.g. حَسَنٌ (beautiful) is a permanent quality, as compared to اِسْمُ الْفَاعِلِ which indicates a temporary meaning e.g. ضَارِبٌ is a temporary quality which exists only at the time of the action.

- All such *isms* which are derived from a اَلثُّلَاثِيُّ اللَّازِمُ (three-letter intransitive *fi'l*) and convey the meaning of اِسْمُ الْفَاعِلِ but are not on the *wazn* of اِسْمُ الْفَاعِلِ, are صِفَةٌ مُشَبَّهَةٌ.

Some of the common *wazns* of صِفَةٌ مُشَبَّهَةٌ (based on usage) are given below

Table 4.8

أَوْزَانُ الصِّفَةِ الْمُشَبَّهَةِ

Wazns	Examples	
	Arabic	Meaning
فَعِلٌ	فَرِحٌ	happy
فَعَلٌ	حَسَنٌ	beautiful
فَعِيلٌ	شَرِيفٌ	noble/honorable
فَعَالٌ	جَبَانٌ	coward
فُعَالٌ	شُجَاعٌ	brave

- Colors and bodily defects appear on the following *wazns*:

  أَفْعَلُ   (masculine)   e.g.   أَحْمَرُ   red

                                             أَبْكَمُ   mute

  فَعْلَاءُ   (feminine)   e.g.   حَمْرَاءُ   red

                                             بَكْمَاءُ   mute

---

[68] For more details, examples, and exercises, please refer to *al-Nahw al-Wadih, Thanawiyyah*, vol. 2, 83-91.

- The اِسْمُ الْفَاعِلِ of non-three letter *fi'l*s (غَيْرُ الثُّلَاثِيّ الْمُجَرَّدِ) is on the *wazn* of its صِفَةٌ مُشَبَّهَةٌ on the condition that permanency of meaning is intended.

    e.g.   مُسْتَقِيمٌ   straight

EXERCISE

1. Translate, fill in the *i'raab*, and identify all the صِفَةٌ مُشَبَّهَةٌ in the following passage.

كان هارون الرشيد فصيحاً كريماً، هُماماً ورِعاً، يحج سنة ويغزو سنة وكان أديباً فطناً، حافظاً للقرآن، سليم الذوق، صحيح التمييز، جريئاً في الحق، مهيباً عند الخاصة والعامة، وكان طلق المحيا، يحب الشعراء ويعطيهم العطاء الجزيل ويدني منه أهل الأدب والدين، ويتواضع للعلماء.

2. Translate, fill in the *i'raab* and identify the *seeghah*s of مُبَالَغَةٌ and اِسْمُ الْفَاعِلِ.

قال حكيم: المؤمن صبُور شكور لا نمّام ولا حسُود ولا حقُود ولا مختال. يطلب من الخيرات أعلاها ومن الأخلاق أسناها. لا يرد سائلا ولا يبخل بمال، متواصل الهمم، مترادف الإحسان، وزّان لكلامه، خزّان للسانه، محسن عمله، مكثر في الحق أمله، ليس بهياب عند الفزع ولا وثاب عند الطمع، مواس للفقراء، رحيم بالضعفاء.

131

<u>Section 4.3.5</u>[69]

اِسْمُ التَّفْضِيْلِ – Comparative and superlative *isms*

<u>Definition:</u> It is an اِسْمٌ which indicates that a quality described by the root letters is found to a greater extent in one person/thing when compared to another.

e.g. خَالِدٌ أَكْبَرُ مِنْ عَمْرٍو Khalid is older/bigger than 'Amr.

It can also refer to the highest degree (superlative) of the quality described by the root letters.

e.g. اَللهُ أَكْبَرُ Allah is the greatest.

<u>Note:</u> This is the case when it is used without مِنْ, i.e. without comparison.

Table 4.9
أَوْزَانُ اِسْمِ التَّفْضِيْلِ

	Masculine	Example	Feminine	Example	Meaning
Singular	أَفْعَلُ	أَكْبَرُ	فُعْلَى	كُبْرَى	Bigger/older
Dual	أَفْعَلَانِ	أَكْبَرَانِ	فُعْلَيَانِ	كُبْرَيَانِ	Bigger/older
Plural	أَفْعَلُوْنَ	أَكْبَرُوْنَ	فُعْلَيَاتٌ	كُبْرَيَاتٌ	Bigger/older
	أَفَاعِلُ	أَكَابِرُ	فُعَلٌ	كُبَرٌ	Bigger/older

<u>Usage:</u>

اِسْمُ التَّفْضِيْلِ is used in three ways.

1. With مِنْ: the اِسْمُ التَّفْضِيْلِ will always be a singular masculine (وَاحِدٌ مُذَكَّرٌ).

    e.g. زَيْدٌ أَعْلَمُ مِنْ بَكْرٍ Zayd is more knowledgeable than Bakr.

    عَائِشَةُ أَكْبَرُ مِنْ زَيْنَبَ 'Aishah is older than Zaynab.

2. With ال: the اِسْمُ التَّفْضِيْلِ must correspond with the word before it in gender and number.

    e.g. اَلزَّيْدَانِ الْأَعْلَمَانِ غَائِبَانِ The two more knowledgeable Zayds are absent.

    عَائِشَةُ الْكُبْرَى حَاضِرَةٌ The older 'Aishah is present.

3. With إِضَافَةٌ: the اِسْمُ التَّفْضِيْلِ may be وَاحِدٌ مُذَكَّرٌ or it may correspond with the word before it.

    e.g. اَلزَّيْدُوْنَ أَعْلَمُو الْقَوْمِ The Zayds are the most knowledgeable of people.

---

[69] For more details, examples, and exercises, please refer to *al-Nahw al-Wadih, Thanawiyyah*, vol. 2, 92-100.

اَلزَّيْدَانِ أَعْلَمَا الْقَوْمِ   اَلزَّيْدَانِ أَعْلَمُ الْقَوْمِ

The two Zayds are the most knowledgeable of people.

عَائِشَةُ كُبْرَى النَّاسِ   عَائِشَةُ أَكْبَرُ النَّاسِ

'Aishah is the oldest of people.

Notes:

1. اِسْمُ التَّفْضِيلِ of words which indicate color, physical defects and of fi'ls غَيْرُ الثُّلَاثِيّ الْمُجَرَّدِ is made by placing the words أَكْثَرُ, أَشَدُّ, etc. before the مَصْدَرٌ of that word. The مَصْدَرٌ will be the تَمْيِيزٌ, and therefore, will be مَنْصُوبٌ.

e.g.   هُوَ أَشَدُّ حُمْرَةً مِنْ زَيْدٍ   He is redder than Zayd.

        هُوَ أَشَدُّ عَرَجًا مِنْ زَيْدٍ   He is lamer than Zayd.

        هُوَ أَكْثَرُ اِجْتِهَادًا مِنْ زَيْدٍ   He is more hard-working than Zayd.

2. The words خَيْرٌ and شَرٌّ are also used for اِسْمُ التَّفْضِيلِ.

e.g.   اَلظَّالِمُ شَرُّ النَّاسِ   The oppressor is the worst of people.

3. اِسْمُ التَّفْضِيلِ gives رَفْعٌ to its hidden ضَمِيرٌ.

e.g.   زَيْدٌ أَفْضَلُ مِنْ بَكْرٍ   Zayd is more virtuous than Bakr.

The *dameer* هُوَ in أَفْضَلُ is its فَاعِلٌ.

EXERCISE

1. Translate, fill in the *i'raab* and explain the usage of اِسْمُ التَّفْضِيلِ in the following sentences.

i. بعض الحيوانات أقوى من الإنسان   v. النساء الفضليات

ii. الأنبياء أفضل الناس   vi. الأنبياء أفاضل الناس

iii. مريم فضلى النساء   vii. الرجلان الأفضلان

iv. أولئك هم خير البرية   viii. ثوبك أشد سوادا من ثوبي

<u>Section 4.3.6</u>[70]

اَلْمَصْدَرُ – Infinitive/verbal *ism*

<u>Definition:</u> It is an اِسْمٌ which refers to the action indicated by the corresponding *fi'l* without any reference to time. It is the root of all derived words (مُشْتَقَّاتٌ).

<u>Effect:</u> It has the same effect as that of its فِعْلٌ i.e. it gives رَفْعٌ to the فَاعِلٌ and نَصْبٌ to the مَفْعُوْلٌ بِهِ.

e.g.   رَأَيْتُ ضَرْباً الْيَوْمَ زَيْدٌ بَكْرًا   Today, I saw Zayd's beating of Bakr.

<u>Usage:</u>

Masdar is generally used in one of the following two ways:

- as a مُضَافٌ to its فَاعِلٌ.

  e.g.   كَرِهْتُ ضَرْبَ زَيْدٍ بَكْرًا   i.e.   (أَنْ يَضْرِبَ زَيْدٌ بَكْرًا)   I disliked Zayd's beating of Bakr.

- as a مُضَافٌ to its مَفْعُوْلٌ بِهِ.

  e.g.   كَرِهْتُ ضَرْبَ بَكْرٍ زَيْدٌ   i.e.   (أَنْ يَضْرِبَ بَكْرًا زَيْدٌ)   I disliked Zayd's beating of Bakr.

EXERCISE

1. Fill in the *i'raab* and explain the usage of the *masdar* in the following sentences.

   i. سرني قراءة رشيد القرآن   iii. إكرام العرب الضيف معروف

   ii. حبك الشيء يعمي ويصم   iv. ولله على الناس حج البيت من استطاع إليه سبيلا

---

[70] For more details, examples, and exercises, please refer to *al-Nahw al-Wadih*, *Thanawiyyah*, vol. 2, 52-70.

اَلْمُضَافُ

In the case of مُضَافٌ, it is assumed that one of the following prepositions (حُرُوْفُ جَرٍّ) is hidden between the مُضَافٌ and مُضَافٌ إِلَيْهِ.

- مِنْ   when the مُضَافٌ إِلَيْهِ is a part/type (جِنْسٌ) of the مُضَافٌ.

  e.g.   خَاتَمٌ فِضَّةٍ   i.e.   خَاتَمٌ مِنْ فِضَّةٍ   silver ring

- فِيْ   when the مُضَافٌ إِلَيْهِ is a ظَرْفٌ.

  e.g.   صَلَاةُ اللَّيْلِ   i.e.   صَلَاةٌ فِي اللَّيْلِ   night prayer

- لِ   when it is neither of the above two.

  e.g.   اِبْنُ زَيْدٍ   i.e.   اِبْنٌ لِزَيْدٍ   Zayd's son

Section 4.3.8

اَلْاِسْمُ التَّامُّ

Definition: It is an اِسْمٌ which gives the *ism* (تَمْيِيْز) after it a *nasb*.

- An اِسْمٌ will be considered as تَامٌّ when it has one of the following:

  a. *tanween*.

  e.g.   مَا فِي السَّمَاءِ قَدْرُ رَاحَةٍ سَحَابًا   (رَاحَةٍ)

  There is not even a palm's measure of clouds in the sky.

  b. hidden *tanween*.

  e.g.   مَعِيْ أَحَدَ عَشَرَ رَجُلًا   (أَحَدٌ وَعَشْرٌ was originally أَحَدَ عَشَرَ)

  There are eleven men with me.

  c. ن of a dual اِسْمٌ.

  e.g.   عِنْدِيْ قَفِيْزَانِ بُرًّا   (قَفِيْزَانِ)

  I have two *qafeezes*[72] of wheat.

  d. ن which resembles the ن of a sound masculine plural (جَمْعُ مُذَكَّرٍ سَالِمٌ).

  e.g.   عِنْدِيْ عِشْرُوْنَ دِرْهَمًا   (عِشْرُوْنَ)

  I have twenty *dirhams*.

The اَلْاِسْمُ التَّامُّ in the above examples cannot be مُضَافٌ while having a *tanween* or having a *noon* of dual/plural, thus the اِسْمٌ after it gets a نَصْبٌ because of it being تَمْيِيْز.

---

[71] For more details, examples, and exercises, please refer to *al-Nahw al-Wadih*, Thanawiyyah, vol. 1, 131-141.

[72] A *qafeez* is a classical Islamic measure of volume. According to the Hanafis, it is equal to 40.344 litres.

<u>Section 4.3.9</u>[73]

<u>اَلْكِنَايَاتُ</u>

<u>Definition:</u> It is an اِسْمٌ which indicates an unspecified quantity.

- It is clarified by the اِسْمٌ following it.
- These are كَمْ and كَذَا.

كَمْ : can be used in two ways: as an interrogative (اِسْتِفْهَامٌ) or as an informative exclamation (خَبَرِيَّةٌ).

1. كَمْ اَلْاِسْتِفْهَامِيَّةُ – (how many)

- It gives the *ism* (تَمْيِيزٌ) after it a نَصْبٌ.
- The تَمْيِيزٌ is singular.

   e.g.   كَمْ كِتَابًا عِنْدَكَ   How many books do you have?

- At times, the preposition مِنْ appears before the تَمْيِيزٌ.

   e.g.   كَمْ مِنْ كِتَابٍ عِنْدَكَ   How many books do you have?

2. كَمْ اَلْخَبَرِيَّةُ – (so many)

- It gives the *ism* (تَمْيِيزٌ) after it a جَرٌّ (because of it being a مُضَافٌ إِلَيْهِ).
- The تَمْيِيزٌ may be singular or plural.

   e.g.   كَمْ مَالٍ أَنْفَقْتَ   So much of wealth you have spent!

   e.g   كَمْ أَمْوَالٍ أَنْفَقْتَ   So much of wealths you have spent!

- At times the preposition مِنْ appears before the تَمْيِيزٌ.

   e.g.   كَمْ مِنْ مَلَكٍ فِي السَّمٰوٰتِ   There are so many angels in the skies/heavens!

كَذَا – (so much, such and such)

- It gives the *ism* (تَمْيِيزٌ) after it a *nasb*.
- The تَمْيِيزٌ is singular.

   e.g   عِنْدِيْ كَذَا دِرْهَمًا   I have this much *dirhams*.

EXERCISE

1. What is the difference between the following sentences.

   ii. كم كتابٍ قرأت   i. كم كتابا قرأت

---

[73] For more details, examples, and exercises, please refer to *al-Nahw al-Wadih, Thanawiyyah*, vol. 2, 170-173.

Section 4.4

اَلْحُرُوفُ الْغَيْرُ الْعَامِلَةِ – Non-governing particles

1. حُرُوفُ التَّنْبِيْهِ – **Particles of notification:**

These are used to draw the attention of the listener. These are as follows:

أَلَا   أَمَا   هَا   meaning   Lo! / Behold! / Take heed!

e.g.   أَلَا اِنَّ نَصْرَ اللهِ قَرِيْبٌ   Behold! Indeed, Allah's help is near.

أَمَا زَيْدٌ نَائِمٌ   Behold! Zayd is sleeping.

هَا أَنَا حَاضِرٌ   Lo! I am present.

هٰذَا   This

<u>Note:</u> The actual اِسْمُ إِشَارَةٍ is only ذَا, while هَا is the حَرْفُ تَنْبِيْهٍ. However, in common usage the whole is referred to as اِسْمُ إِشَارَةٍ without differentiating.

2. حُرُوفُ الْإِيْجَاب – **Particles of affirmation:**[74]

These are used for affirmation of a statement made earlier. These are as follows:

إِنَّ   جَيْرِ   أَجَلْ   إِيْ   بَلٰى   نَعَمْ

نَعَمْ – (yes)

- It is used to confirm a statement, be it positive or negative. For example,
  - If someone says أَجَاءَ زَيْدٌ؟ (Did Zayd come?), the reply will be نَعَمْ (yes) meaning جَاءَ زَيْدٌ (Zayd came.).
  - If someone says أَمَا جَاءَ زَيْدٌ؟ (Has Zayd not come?), the reply will be نَعَمْ (yes) meaning مَا جَاءَ زَيْدٌ (Zayd did not come.).

بَلٰى – (yes, why not)

- It is used to convert a negative statement into a positive one.

  e.g.   If someone says أَلَمْ يَقُمْ زَيْدٌ؟ (Did Zayd not stand up?), the reply will be بَلٰى (yes, why not) meaning قَدْ قَامَ زَيْدٌ (Zayd has stood up.).

إِيْ – (yes)

- It is the same as نَعَمْ. However it is used with an oath (قَسَمٌ) after a question.

  e.g.   If someone says أَقَامَ زَيْدٌ؟ (Did Zayd stand up?), the reply will be إِيْ وَاللهِ (yes, by Allah!) meaning قَامَ زَيْدٌ (Zayd stood up.).

---

[74] For more examples and exercises, please refer to *al-Nahw al-Wadih, Ibtida'iyyah*, vol. 3, 168-174.

إِنَّ / جَيْرِ / أَجَلْ – (yes)

- These have the same meaning as نَعَمْ.

  e.g.   If someone says أَجَاءَ زَيْدٌ؟ (Did Zayd come?), the reply will be إِنَّ or جَيْرِ or

  أَجَلْ (yes) meaning جَاءَ زَيْدٌ (Zayd came.).

  Note: إِنَّ is very rarely used for this purpose.

3. حَرْفَا التَّفْسِيرِ – Particles of clarification:

These are used to clarify a word in a sentence. These are as follows:

أَيْ   أَنْ   (that is)

e.g.   وَاسْئَلِ الْقَرْيَةَ أَيْ أَهْلَ الْقَرْيَةِ   And ask the town, that is, the people of the

town.

وَنَادَيْنَاهُ أَنْ يَإِبْرَاهِيمُ   And We called him, that is, O Ibraheem!

4. اَلْحُرُوفُ الْمَصْدَرِيَّةُ: These are used to give a *masdari* meaning. These are as follows:

أَنَّ   أَنْ   مَا

- مَا and أَنْ come before a جُمْلَةٌ فِعْلِيَّةٌ.

- أَنَّ comes before a جُمْلَةٌ اِسْمِيَّةٌ.

e.g.   حَتَّى إِذَا ضَاقَتْ عَلَيْهِمُ الْأَرْضُ بِمَا رَحُبَتْ (بِرُحْبِهَا)

Until when the earth became straitened for them despite its vastness.

يَسُرُّنِي أَنْ تَصْدُقَ   (صِدْقُكَ)   Your truthfulness pleases me.

بَلَغَنِي أَنَّ زَيْدًا نَائِمٌ   (نَوْمُ زَيْدٍ)   (News of) Zayd's sleeping reached me.

Note: أَنْ and أَنَّ are <u>governing</u> particles.

5. حُرُوفُ التَّحْضِيضِ – Particles of exhortation:

These are used to encourage someone to do something when they appear before فِعْلٌ مُضَارِعٌ.
These are as follows:

لَوْمَا   لَوْلَا   هَلَّا   أَلَا

e.g.   هَلَّا تُصَلِّي؟   Do you not pray *salah*?

- These particles are also used to create regret and sorrow in the listener when they
  appear before فِعْلٌ مَاضٍ. Therefore, they are also called حُرُوفُ التَّنْدِيمِ.

  e.g.   هَلَّا صَلَّيْتَ الْعَصْرَ؟   Have you not prayed '*Asr salah*?

  e.g.   وَلَوْلَا إِذْ سَمِعْتُمُوهُ قُلْتُمْ...   When you heard it, why did you not say...

6. حَرْفُ التَّوَقُّع – **Particle of anticipation:**[75]

This is قَدْ. An example of its usage for تَوَقُّعٌ is as follows.

قَدْ يَقْدُمُ الْغَائِبُ الْيَوْمَ   Probably, the absent person will return today.

- Besides تَوَقُّعٌ, قَدْ can also be used for one or more of the following. These are all more common than its usage for تَوَقُّعٌ.

  تَقْرِيبٌ: In this case, it gives فِعْلٌ مَاضٍ the meaning of near past. This usage is specific to فِعْلٌ مَاضٍ.

  e.g.   قَدْ جَاءَ زَيْدٌ   Zayd has arrived (recently).

  تَقْلِيلٌ: In this case, it gives فِعْلٌ مُضَارِعٌ the meaning of seldomness. This usage is specific to فِعْلٌ مُضَارِعٌ.

  e.g.   إِنَّ الْجَوَادَ قَدْ يَبْخَلُ   Indeed, sometimes, a generous person is miserly.

  تَحْقِيقٌ: In this case, it gives فِعْلٌ مَاضٍ or فِعْلٌ مُضَارِعٌ the meaning of certainty.

  e.g.   قَدْ جَاءَ زَيْدٌ   Certainly, Zayd came.

        قَدْ يَعْلَمُ اللهُ   Certainly, Allah knows.

- قَدْ can also be used simultaneously for more than one of the above-mentioned purposes. An example of قَدْ being simultaneously used for تَوَقُّعٌ, تَقْرِيبٌ, and تَحْقِيقٌ, is as follows:

  قَدْ قَامَتِ الصَّلَاةُ   Indeed, *salah* has been established/is about to be established.

Note: لَعَلَّ can also be used for تَوَقُّعٌ.

7. حَرْفَا الْاِسْتِفْهَام – **Particles of interrogation:**[76]

These are أ and هَلْ.

e.g.   أَزَيْدٌ قَائِمٌ؟   Is Zayd standing?

      هَلْ قَامَ زَيْدٌ؟   Did Zayd stand up?

---

[75] This is based on *Mu'jam al-Qawa'id al-'Arabiyyah*. See *Mu'jam al-Qawa'id al-'Arabiyyah*, 338-339.

[76] For more examples, and exercises, please refer to *al-Nahw al-Wadih, Ibtida'iyyah*, vol. 3, 168-171.

8. حَرْفُ الرَّدْعِ – **Particle of rebuke:**

This is كَلَّا, which means "Never!"

- It can be used to rebuke or reprimand.

  e.g.   كَلَّا   said in response to someone who says اِضْرِبْ زَيْدًا (Hit Zayd.).

- It can also be used to convey the meaning of certainty.

  e.g.   كَلَّا سَوْفَ تَعْلَمُوْنَ   Indeed, soon you will know.

  <u>Note:</u> This is according to one translation. According to another, it is in the meaning of "never."

9. اَلتَّنْوِيْنُ: It is used for one or more of the following:

  تَمَكُّنٌ: It is a *tanween* which shows an *ism* to be مُعْرَبٌ.

  e.g.   زَيْدٌ

  تَنْكِيْرٌ: It is a *tanween* which shows an *ism* to be نَكِرَةٌ.

  e.g.   رَجُلٌ

  تَعْوِيْضٌ: It is a *tanween* which subsitutes a مُضَافٌ إِلَيْهِ.

  e.g.   يَوْمَئِذٍ   i.e.   يَوْمَ إِذَا كَانَ كَذَا   the day when such and such happens

10. نُوْنُ التَّأْكِيْدِ: It is used for emphasis in مُضَارِعٌ, أَمْرٌ and نَهْيٌ. It is of two forms: ثَقِيْلَةٌ and خَفِيْفَةٌ. Both have the same meaning.

اَلثَّقِيْلَةُ (نّ)	اَلْخَفِيْفَةُ (نْ)	
لَيَضْرِبَنَّ	لَيَضْرِبَنْ	Indeed, he should hit.
أُنْصُرَنَّ	أُنْصُرَنْ	You must help.

11. حَرْفُ لَ: It can be used for the following:

  اِبْتِدَاءٌ: It appears before the مُبْتَدَأٌ and is used for emphasis.

  e.g.   لَأَنْتُمْ أَشَدُّ رَهْبَةً   Indeed, you are more feared.

  جَوَابٌ: It comes in the answer to لَوْ – لَوْلَا and قَسَمٌ.

  e.g.   وَلَوْلَا دَفْعُ اللهِ النَّاسَ بَعْضَهُمْ بِبَعْضٍ لَفَسَدَتِ الْأَرْضُ

  If Allah did not repel some people by means of others, the earth would be corrupted.

  وَاللهِ لَأَصُوْمَنَّ غَدًا   By Allah! I will fast tommorrow.

  زَائِدَةٌ: This is extra and can be used for emphasis.

  e.g.   إِنَّهُمْ لَيَأْكُلُوْنَ الطَّعَامَ   Indeed, they eat food.

140

12. اَلْحُرُوفُ الزَّائِدَةُ – __Extra particles:__ These are not translated. However, they add beauty and emphasis to the meaning. They may also stop the effect (عَمَلٌ) of an عَامِلٌ. These are:

إِنْ   أَنْ   مَا   لَا   لَ   مِنْ   كَ   بِ   (عَامِلَةٌ – ب، كَ، مِنْ) are governing particles

__Usage:__

إِنْ: It appears after مَا اَلنَّافِيَةُ.

e.g.   مَا إِنْ زَيْدٌ قَائِمٌ   Zayd is not standing.

أَنْ: It appears after لَمَّا.

e.g.   فَلَمَّا أَنْ جَاءَ الْبَشِيرُ   When the bearer of good news came.

مَا: It appears after the following:

| إِذَا | e.g. | إِذَا مَا ابْتُلِيتَ فَاصْبِرْ | When you are afflicted, be patient. |

| مَتَى | e.g. | مَتَى مَا تُسَافِرْ أُسَافِرْ | When you travel, I will travel. |

| أَيٌّ | e.g. | أَيَّمَا الرَّجُلُ جَاءَكَ فَأَكْرِمْهُ | Whoever comes to you, treat him hospitably. |

Here, مَا blocked the عَمَل of أَيٌّ.

| أَيْنَ | e.g. | أَيْنَمَا تُوَلُّوا فَثَمَّ وَجْهُ اللهِ | Whichever way you turn, there is the face of Allah. |

| إِنْ | e.g. | فَإِمَّا يَأْتِيَنَّكُمْ مِنِّي هُدًى | Then, should some guidance come to you from Me. |

| حَرْفُ جَرٍّ | e.g. | فَبِمَا رَحْمَةٍ مِّنَ اللهِ لِنْتَ لَهُمْ | So, it is through mercy from Allah that you are gentle to them. |

Here, مَا did not block the عَمَل of حَرْفُ جَرٍّ.

| لَا | e.g. | لَا أُقْسِمُ بِهَذَا الْبَلَدِ | I swear by this city. |

| لَ | e.g. | إِنَّهُمْ لَيَأْكُلُونَ الطَّعَامَ | Indeed, they eat food. |

| مِنْ | e.g. | هَلْ مِنْ خَالِقٍ غَيْرُ اللهِ؟ | Is there a creator besides Allah? |

| كَ | e.g. | لَيْسَ كَمِثْلِهِ شَيْءٌ | There is nothing like Him. |

| بِ | e.g. | لَيْسَ زَيْدٌ بِكَاذِبٍ | Zayd is not a liar. |

13. حُرُوفُ الشَّرْطِ الَّتِيْ لَا تَجْزِمُ – Conditional particles that do not cause *jazm*:[77]

أَمَّا (however, as for, as far as…is concerned)

- It is used to explain/clarify something, which was mentioned briefly.
- ف should be used before its answer (جَوَابٌ).

e.g. فَمِنْهُمْ شَقِيٌّ وَسَعِيْدٌ فَأَمَّا الَّذِيْنَ شَقُوْا فَفِي النَّارِ

So, some of them will be wretched and (some) blessed. As for the wretched, they will be in the Fire.

لَوْ (if)

- It is used to negate the second sentence (جَوَابٌ) on account of the first sentence (شَرْطٌ) not being fulfilled.

e.g. لَوْ كَانَ فِيْهِمَا أَلِهَةٌ إِلَّا اللهُ لَفَسَدَتَا

If there had been gods besides Allah in them (the heavens and the earth), they would have been corrupted.
(There will not be corruption because more than one god does not exist.)

<u>Note:</u> If a وَ is added to لَوْ i.e. وَلَوْ, it will give the meaning of "even if/even though" and will be known as لَوْ وَصْلِيَّةٌ.

e.g. أَوْلِمْ وَلَوْ بِشَاةٍ   Celebrate *walimah* even if it be with one (slaughtered) goat.

لَوْمَا and لَوْلَا (if such and such had not been so, …)

- Apart from being used for تَحْضِيْضٌ and تَنْدِيْمٌ, they are also used to demonstrate that the second sentence (جَوَابٌ) cannot be attained because of the presence of the condition of the first sentence (شَرْطٌ).

e.g. لَوْلَا زَيْدٌ لَهَلَكَ بَكْرٌ   Had it not been for Zayd, Bakr would have perished.

لَمَّا (when)

- This is a ظَرْفٌ in the meaning of حِيْنَ. It enters upon فِعْلٌ مَاضٍ.

e.g. لَمَّا سَلَّمْتُ عَلَيْهِ رَدَّ عَلَيَّ السَّلَامَ   When I greeted him, he returned my greeting.

---

[77] For more details, examples, and exercises, please refer to *al-Nahw al-Wadih*, *Thanawiyyah*, vol. 2, 43-48.

14. مَا (مَا دَامَ): It is a مَا which has the meaning of مَا دَامَ (as long as).

e.g. أَقُوْمُ مَا دَامَ الْأَمِيْرُ جَالِساً   i.e.   أَقُوْمُ مَا جَلَسَ الْأَمِيْرُ

I will stand as long as the leader is sitting.

15. حُرُوْفُ الْعَطْفِ: These have been discussed in Section 3.10.4

FINAL EXERCISE

Q: Go through the whole book and identify the various meanings and uses of the following:

أَنْ   إِنْ   لِ   أَيُّ   أَيَّانَ   أَيْنَ   مَتَى   لَمَّا   مَنْ   مَا   لَا

حَتَّى   ف   و   أَنَّ

فَالْحَمْدُ لِلهِ الَّذِيْ بِنِعْمَتِهِ تَتِمُّ الصَّالِحَاتُ

وَالصَّلَاةُ وَالسَّلَامُ عَلَى رَسُوْلِهِ الْكَرِيْمِ وَعَلَى آلِهِ الطَّيِّبِيْنَ الطَّاهِرِيْنَ وَعَلَى أَصْحَابِهِ أَجْمَعِيْنَ

APPENDIX

Studying Classical/Qur'anic Arabic

There are a number of options available for the student of sacred Islamic knowledge seeking to learn classical Arabic on his/her path to learning the *deen*. The following is a set of suggested curricula for studying Arabic language, based upon the South Asian (Indo-Paki) scholarly tradition. It is by no means the only option. To begin with, Urdu texts have been omitted. Moreover, those following other scholarly traditions (Arab, Turkish, South East Asian) may have a somewhat different set of books, although they will also find some overlap here.

The books whose names are only mentioned in English are English texts, while those whose Arabic names are also given are Arabic texts. The texts increase in difficulty and advancement downward.

General Arabic Language

Level	Texts		
Beginner to Intermediate	*Durus al-Lughah al-'Arabiyyah* vols. 1-3 (دُرُوْسُ اللُّغَةِ الْعَرَبِيَّةِ) OR *Al-'Arabiyyah Bayna Yadayka* vols. 1-3 (الْعَرَبِيَّةُ بَيْنَ يَدَيْكَ)	*Arabic Tutor* vols. 1-2	*Ten Lessons of Arabic*

Nahw

Level	Texts
Beginner to Intermediate	*Tasheel al-Nahw*
	Sharh Mi'at 'Amil (شَرْحُ مِائَةِ عَامِلٍ) OR *'Awamil al-Nahw* (عَوَامِلُ النَّحْوِ)
	Hidayat al-Nahw (هِدَايَةُ النَّحْوِ) OR *Al-Ajurrumiyyah* (الْآجُرُّوْمِيَّةُ) with commentary *al-Tuhfah al-Saniyyah* (التُّحْفَةُ السَّنِيَّةُ)
	Al-Kafiyah (الْكَافِيَةُ)
Advanced	*Sharh ibn 'Aqil* (شَرْحُ ابْنِ عَقِيْلٍ) OR *Sharh Jami* (شَرْحُ الْجَامِيْ) OR *Sharh Qatr al-Nada wa Ball al-Sada* (شَرْحُ قَطْرِ النَّدَى وَبَلُّ الصَّدَى) OR *Sharh Shudhur al-Dhahab* (شَرْحُ شُذُوْرِ الذَّهَبِ)

The texts *al-Nahw al-Wadih li al-Madaris al-Ibtida'iyyah* vols. 1-3 (اَلنَّحْوُ الْوَاضِحُ لِلْمَدَارِسِ الْإِبْتِدَائِيَّةِ) and *al-Nahw al-Wadih li al-Madaris al-Thanawiyyah* vols. 1-3 (اَلنَّحْوُ الْوَاضِحُ لِلْمَدَارِسِ الثَّانَوِيَّةِ) belong to the intermediate to advanced level. The six volumes in general, and the three *al-Ibtida'iyyah* volumes in particular, can be used in place of, or in conjunction with *Tasheel al-Nahw*. The six could also be used in conjunction with *Hidayat al-Nahw*. Almost always, one of these texts has something that the other does not.

Sarf

Level	Texts
Beginner	*Fundamentals of Classical Arabic* vol. 1
Intermediate	*From the Treasures of Arabic Morphology*
	'Ilm al-Seeghah (عِلْمُ الصِّيغَةِ) OR
	Shadha al-'Arf fi Fann al-Sarf (شَذَا الْعَرْفِ فِي فَنِّ الصَّرْفِ)

Arabic Reading/Literature

Level	Texts	
Beginner	*Al-Qira'ah al-Rashidah* vol. 1 (اَلْقِرَاءَةُ الرَّاشِدَةُ)	*Qasas al-Nabiyyin* vol. 1 (قَصَصُ النَّبِيِّينَ)
		Qasas al-Nabiyyin vol. 2 (قَصَصُ النَّبِيِّينَ)
		Qasas al-Nabiyyin vol. 3 (قَصَصُ النَّبِيِّينَ)
Intermediate	*Al-Qira'ah al-Rashidah* vol. 2 (اَلْقِرَاءَةُ الرَّاشِدَةُ)	*Qasas al-Nabiyyin* vol. 4 (قَصَصُ النَّبِيِّينَ)
	Nafhat al-'Arab (نَفْحَةُ الْعَرَبِ)	*Qasas al-Nabiyyin* vol. 5 (قَصَصُ النَّبِيِّينَ)
Advanced	*Mukhtarat min Adab al-'Arab* vol. 1 (مُخْتَارَاتٌ مِنْ أَدَبِ الْعَرَبِ)	*Al-Maqamat al-Haririyyah* (اَلْمَقَامَاتُ الْحَرِيرِيَّةُ)
	Mukhtarat min Adab al-'Arab vol. 2 (مُخْتَارَاتٌ مِنْ أَدَبِ الْعَرَبِ)	

Arabic Rhetoric (*Balaghah*)

Level	Texts
Beginner	*Durus al-Balaghah* (دُرُوسُ الْبَلَاغَةِ)
Intermediate to Advanced	*Al-Balaghah al-Wadihah* (اَلْبَلَاغَةُ الْوَاضِحَةُ)
	Talkhees al-Miftah (تَلْخِيصُ الْمِفْتَاحِ)
	OR
	its commentary *Mukhtasar al-Ma'ani* (مُخْتَصَرُ الْمَعَانِيْ)

Suggested Curriculum

Below, we have provided a suggested curriculum based upon some of the texts given above that could be followed as part of an overall traditional Arabic & Islamic Studies curriculum. This curriculum is based on a two-semester academic year.

Year	Sem	Texts				
1	1	*Ten Lessons of Arabic*	*Fundamentals* vol. 1	*Durus al-Lughah* vol. 1		
1	2	*Tasheel al-Nahw* (using *Al-Nahw al-Wadih Ibtida'iyyah* & *Thanawiyyah* for reference/examples)	*Treasures of Arabic Morphology*	*Durus al-Lughah* vol. 1 (continued if not completed, followed by vol. 2)	*Arabic Tutor* vol. 1	*Qasas al-Nabiyyin* vols. 1 & 2
2	1	*Tasheel al-Nahw* (continued, if not yet completed) followed by selected readings & exercises from *al-Nahw al-Wadih Ibtida'iyyah* & *Thanawiyyah*	*Treasures of Arabic Morphology* (continued)	*Durus al-Lughah* vol. 2 (continued if not yet completed, followed by vol. 3)	*Arabic Tutor* vol. 1 (continued if not yet completed, followed by vol. 2)	*Qasas al-Nabiyyin* vols. 3 & 4
2	2	*Hidayat al-Nahw* / *'Awaamil al-Nahw* OR *Sharh Mi'at 'Aamil*	*'Ilm al-Seeghah*		*Nafhat al-'Arab*	*Qasas al-Nabiyyin* vol. 5
3	1	*Sharh ibn 'Aqil* vol. 1	*Durus al-Balaghah*			*Mukhtarat* vol. 1
3	2	*Sharh ibn 'Aqil* vol. 1	*Durus al-Balaghah* (continued, if not yet completed) followed by selected readings from *Talkhees al-Miftah* OR its commentary *Mukhtasar al-Ma'ani*			*Mukhtarat* vol. 1

BIBLIOGRAPHY

Kidwai, ʿAbd al-Salam and Aamir Bashir. (2016). *Ten Lessons of Arabic*. Chicago: Dār al-Saʿādah Publications.

ʿAbd al-Ghaniyy al-Daqr. (1986). *Muʿjam al-Qawaʿid al-ʿArabiyyah fi al-Nahw wa al-Tasreef* [Handbook of Arabic Grammar Rules]. Damascus: Dar al-Qalam.

ʿAbd al-Majid Nadvi. (n.d.). Vol. 1, *Muʿallim al-Insha'* [Composition Tutor]. Karachi: Majlis Nashriat-e-Islam.

ʿAbd al-Rahman al-Fawzan, Mukhtar Husayn & Muhammad ʿAbd al-Khaliq. (2007). *Al-ʿArabiyyah bayna Yadayk* [Arabic Before You] *(Vols. 1-3)*. Riyadh: Al-ʿArabiyyah li al-Jameeʿ.

ʿAbd al-Sattar Khan. (2007). *Arabic Tutor (Vols. 1-2)* (Ebrahim Muhammad, Trans.). Camperdown, South Africa: Madrasah Inʿamiyyah.

ʿAbdullah ibn ʿAqil. (1980). *Sharh ibn ʿAqil ʿala Alfiyyat ibn Malik* [Ibn ʿAqil's Commentary on *The One-thousand Verse Poem* of Ibn Malik] *(Vols. 1-4)*. Cairo: Dar al-Turath.

Abul Hasan ʿAli al-Nadwi. (n.d.). *Al-Qira'ah al-Rashidah* [The Rightly Guided Reading] *(Vols. 1-2)*. Karachi: Majlis Nashriat-e-Islam.

Abul Hasan ʿAli al-Nadwi. (n.d.). *Mukhtarat min Adab al-ʿArab* [Selections from the Literature of the Arabs] *(Vols. 1-2)*. Karachi: Majlis Nashriat-e-Islam.

Abul Hasan ʿAli al-Nadwi. (n.d.). *Qasas al-Nabiyyin* [Stories of the Prophets] *(Vols. 1-5)*. Karachi: Majlis Nashriat-e-Islam.

ʿAli al-Jaarim & Mustafa Ameen. (n.d.). *Al-Balaghah al-Wadihah* [Clear Rhetoric]. Cairo: Dar al-Maʿarif.

ʿAli al-Jaarim & Mustafa Ameen. (n.d.). *Al-Nahw al-Wadih li al-Madaris al-Ibtida'iyyah* [Clear Grammar for Elementary Schools], *(Vols. 1-3)*. Cairo: Dar al-Maʿarif.

ʿAli al-Jaarim & Mustafa Ameen. (n.d.). *Al-Nahw al-Wadih li al-Madaris al-Thanawiyyah* [Clear Grammar for Secondary Schools], *(Vols. 1-3)*. Cairo: Dar al-Maʿarif.

Al-Andalusi, ibn Hayyan. (2008). *Hidayat al-Nahw* [Guide to Grammar]. Karachi: Maktabat al-Bushra.

Al-Ansari, Abdullah ibn Hisham. (1994). *Sharh Qatr al-Nada wa Ball al-Sada* [Commentary on *The Drops of Dew and the Moisture of Thirst*], with notes by Muhammad Muhy al-Din ʿAbd al-Hamid. Beirut: al-Maktabah al-ʿAsariyyah.

Al-Ansari, Abdullah ibn Hisham. (1990). *Sharh Shudhur al-Dhahab* [Commentary on *The Scattered Particles of Gold*]. Beirut: Maktabat Lubnan.

Al-Hamlawi, Ahmad ibn Muhammad. (2005). Muhammad ibn ‘Abd al-Mu‘ti (ed.). *Shadha al-‘Arf fi Fann al-Sarf* [Strong Fragrance Regarding the Science of Morphology]. Riyadh: Dar al-Kayan.

Al-Hariri, Muhammad al-Qasim ibn ‘Ali. (n.d.). *Al-Maqamat al-Haririyyah* [The Assemblies of al-Hariri]. Lahore: Maktabah Rahmaniyyah.

Al-Jurjani, ‘Abd al-Qahir. (n.d.). *Sharh Mi’at ‘Amil* [Commentary of Hundred Governing Words]. Karachi: Qadimi Kutubkhana.

Al-Qazwini, Muhammad ibn ‘Abd al-Rahman. (2010). *Talkhees al-Miftah* [Summary of *The Key*]. Karachi: Maktabat al-Bushra.

Al-Taftazani, Mas‘ood ibn ‘Umar. (2010). *Mukhtasar al-Ma‘ani* [Summary of Rhetoric]. Karachi: Maktabat al-Bushra.

Charthawali, Mawlana Mushtaq Ahmad. (n.d.). *‘Ilm al-Nahw* [Science of Grammar]. Karachi: Altaf & Sons.

Charthawali, Mawlana Mushtaq Ahmad. (2010). *‘Awamil al-Nahw* [Governing Words of Grammar]. Karachi: Maktabat al-Bushra.

Dockrat, Mawlana Hasan. (2003). *Tawdeeh al-Nahw: A Simplified Arabic Grammar*. Azaadville, South Africa: Madrasah Arabiah Islamia.

Ebrahim Muhammad. (2006). *From the Treasures of Arabic Morphology*. Camperdown, South Africa: Madrasah In‘amiyyah.

Husain Abdul Sattar. (2002). Vol. 1, *Fundamentals of Classical Arabic*. Chicago: Faqir Publications.

Ibn al-Hajib. (2008). *Al-Kafiyah* [The Sufficient]. Karachi: Maktabat al-Bushra.

Jami, ‘Abd al-Rahman. (2011). *Sharh al-Mulla al-Jami ‘ala al-Kafiyah* [The Commentary of Mulla Jami on *The Sufficient*]. Karachi: Maktabat al-Bushra.

Lane, E. W. (1968). Book I, Parts 4-6, *An Arabic-English Lexicon*. Beirut: Librairie du Liban.

Muhammad Diyab, Sultan Muhammad, et. al. (2009). *Durus al-Balaghah* [Lessons of Rhetoric]. Karachi: Maktabat al-Bushra.

Muhammad ‘Inayat Ahmad. (n.d.). *‘Ilm al-Seeghah* [Science of Forms]. (Wali Khan al-Muzaffar, Trans.). Karachi: al-Maktabah al-Faruqiyyah.

Muhammad I‘zaz ‘Ali. (2010). *Nafhat al-‘Arab* [Fragrance of the Arabs]. Karachi: Maktabat al-Bushra.

Muhammad Muhy al-Din ‘Abd al-Hamid. (1989). *Al-Tuhfah al-Saniyyah bi Sharh Muqaddamat al-Ajurrumiyyah* [The Sublime Gift of Commentary on the *Ajurrumi Prolegomena*]. Cairo: Maktabat al-Sunnah

V. ‘Abd al-Rahim. (2009). *Durus al-Lughah al-‘Arabiyyah* [Lessons of Arabic Language], *(Vols. 1-3)*. Chennai: Islamic Foundation.

OUR PUBLICATIONS

Tasheel al-Nahw
Version 2.2

Al-Tamarin Al-Nahwiyyah
Nahw Workbook

Arabic Vocabulary Booklet

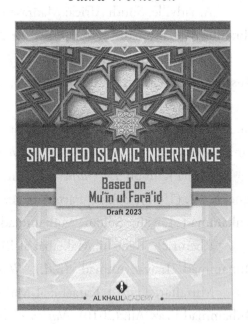

Simplified Islamic Inheritance

US	UK	Canada

Made in the USA
Monee, IL
11 September 2024